... Gorman is an award-winning comedian, storyteller and writer. He has numerous TV writing credits and was part of the double BAFTA-winning team behind *The Mrs Merton Show*. His live shows have won many awards and he is the only performer to twice win the Jury Prize for Best One Person Show at the prestigious HBO US Comedy Arts Festival. He was the host of *Genius*, which ran for three series on Radio 4 and then two series on BBC2. He has appeared in numerous other TV shows, including *Absolutely Fabulous*, *The Frank Skinner Show*, *Late Show with David Letterman*, *The Tonight Show with Jay Leno* and *The Daily Show with Jon Stewart*. His documentary film, *America Unchained*, won the Audience Award for Best Documentary Feature at the Austin Film Festival. His 2013 TV show, *Modern Life Is Goodish*, made for UKTV's Dave channel, saw him dissecting the foibles of modern life in six hour-long comic performances. It quickly established itself as the channel's most successful original programme that year and a further sixteen episodes have been commissioned for broadcast in 2014 and 2015. He'll probably be stealing bits of this book for some of them. His ambition is to one day become a team captain on *Call My Bluff*.

www.davegorman.com

Also by Dave Gorman:

Are You Dave Gorman?
Dave Gorman's Googlewhack Adventure
America Unchained
Dave Gorman vs. The Rest of the World

TOO MUCH INFORMATION

...OR CAN EVERYONE JUST SHUT UP FOR A MOMENT,
SOME OF US ARE TRYING TO THINK.

DAVE GORMAN

EBURY
PRESS

3 5 7 9 10 8 6 4 2

Ebury Press, an imprint of Ebury Publishing,
20 Vauxhall Bridge Road,
London SW1V 2SA

Ebury Press is part of the Penguin Random House group of companies
whose addresses can be found at global.penguinrandomhouse.com

Copyright © Dave Gorman 2014

Dave Gorman has asserted his right to be identified as the author of this
Work in accordance with the Copyright, Designs and Patents Act 1988

First published by Ebury Press in 2014
This edition published by Ebury Press in 2015

www.eburypublishing.co.uk

A CIP catalogue record for this book is available from the British Library

ISBN 9780091928506

Printed and bound by
CPI Group (UK) Ltd, Croydon, CR0 4YY

For Steve.
He was a damn fine squirrel.

CONTENTS

• • • • • • • • • • • •

ACKNOWLEDGEMENTS

Huge thanks to Jake Lingwood, Liz Marvin, Susan Pegg and everyone at Ebury, especially the citizens of the People's Republic of Mondeo. Thanks to Rob Aslett, Cat Gray, Dan Lloyd and all at Avalon, too. Thanks to Duncan Soar for the photos and to David Eldridge at Two Associates for knowing what to do with them.

Martin A. Brooks and Orlando Scott-Cowley were incredibly generous with their time and their wisdom – I'm very grateful to them both. But my biggest thanks must go to my wife, Beth, whose boundless support, understanding and constancy mean the world to me.

AUTHOR'S NOTE

Where appropriate, I've sprinkled a few internet links around in the footnotes. I've tried to generate short codes with obvious derivations in order to make them memorable should anyone want to re-type them into their browser. But do bear in mind that they are links to pages I do not control and so I can't offer any guarantee that the pages in question will exist for all time. If a newspaper website edits or removes a page or a YouTube video is taken down for some reason ... well, that's the nature of the internet. It's beyond my control. But please trust me – they *were* there!

'There are many things of which a wise man might wish to be ignorant'

Ralph Waldo Emerson

CHAPTER 1

. . . .

TOO MUCH INFORMATION

nformation is addictive. It is everywhere and yet I cannot get enough. I must suckle on the teat of the world wide web. I get twitchy if it is withheld.

They say men can't multitask but I can multi-procrastinate. It's damaging my ability to uni-task.

As I type this I am sitting at my desk in the tiny pit of a room I laughingly call my office. I'm trying to focus on the Word document where these words are slowly emerging but the largely blank expanse of bright white pixels is struggling to hold my attention because poking out from behind it – like a crowd of gurning loons that's gathered behind a local news reporter on an outside broadcast – are various windows of distraction.

I'm logged on to a football club website because there are rumours of an imminent transfer and I don't want to miss an announcement. A second window is logged on to the BBC news page. Facebook occupies a third.

I can check for new emails in a snap and I'm also monitoring Twitter on an application called TweetDeck

– an onscreen dashboard of various columns that constantly update as activity occurs. Which it does often. Every few seconds in fact. TweetDeck looks like a stock trader's computer screen when the markets are on fire. '*Buy "whimsy". Sell "rage".*'

No matter how urgent the demands of my Word document, I know that behind it there is *always* something new I can look at. Something stimulating. New news. New newness. Let me suckle at that teat. I mean, I could leave it until later … but then I'll miss something and I can't risk missing something. I must see everything. Ten-minute-old news? Not for me. I don't want stale news. I want fresh news. And fresh cat videos too for that matter.

*

Here's a bit of 1990s trivia for you: *Some of the people born in the 1990s are now adults.*

I find it hard to believe myself but I've checked it with a calculator and there's no getting away from it. It's a fact. And it'll be even factier tomorrow.

If you're one of them then this world is pretty much all you've known. This world of constant connection – this incessant swarm of data – is the world you were born into.

I am not one of them. I am an old man. I am a dinosaur. I grew up in a simpler age.

I was explaining to one of my nieces recently that for the first six years of my life the only television I saw was black and white. She chewed her lip and stared me down, clearly suspicious that I was making things up.

But I wasn't. It was 1977 when my parents finally took the plunge and rented a colour TV. I may have been only six but the arrival of a colour set was so exciting the occasion is burned into my memory as if it were yesterday. Seeing cartoons in colour for the first time blew my tiny mind.

I couldn't understand why my parents weren't as excited by the cartoons as I was. Tennis is what excited them. It was their desire to watch Wimbledon in colour that finally persuaded them to go all high tech. They were very glad they did too as that year saw a rare British Wimbledon win. When Virginia Wade held the Rosewater Dish aloft, the Gorman household didn't need a commentator to tell us her cardigan was pink. We were living the dream.*

'Was your television *really* in black and white?' asked my niece, sceptically.

'Yes.'

'Hmmmm.' She narrowed her eyes. 'And what about your internet? Was that in black and white too?'

'Ha!' I snorted. 'We didn't have the internet back then! Nobody did. Not really.'

---

* Incidentally, my mum bought her first HD TV just a few short weeks before Britain's next Wimbledon triumph arrived courtesy of Andy Murray in 2013. I'm no expert but if the people behind British tennis want to see another player thrive on those hallowed courts I think they should seriously consider buying my mum a 3D TV next.

She gasped.

'I was a grown-up when I first used the internet,' I continued. 'I can remember sending my first email.'

I can too. I was in my early twenties and I'd just gone online for the first time. Eager to know what this email malarkey was all about, I called my friend, Chris: the one person I knew who was already online. (After I'd disconnected the computer in order to free up the phone line, obviously.) I asked Chris to send me an email. He did. (After we'd both put our phones down and reconnected our computers, obviously.)

The first email I ever read went as follows:

Hi Dave. Is your email working? Chris.

I replied: *Yes!*

He replied: *It's good isn't it?*

I replied: *Yes. It's amazing. I'll call you back.*

And then I called him again so that we could discuss how amazing it was that we could communicate with one another that easily. (After we'd … Oh, you get the idea.)

As it happens, Chris is still a dear and close friend to me, but I doubt we've spoken on the phone in over ten years.

*

Other new-media landmarks are just as clearly fixed in my memory. In 1982 I was glued to the box for the start of Britain's fourth TV channel. At eleven years of age I probably wasn't the target audience for Channel 4's first programme – the words and numbers game show, Countdown – but it was new and that made it exciting anyway. Would we ever have five channels? It seemed impossible to imagine such a thing!

Getting my first mobile phone is another clearly defined landmark. I'd resisted getting one at first. It was partly because they were seen as being a bit naff – they were considered the preserve of arrogant estate agents and yuppie twonks at the time – but mainly it was because I was scared of the financial commitment. But then, for the first time in my life, I landed a job that gave me something approaching a regular income – I was part of a small team of writers working on a TV show – and I figured that meant I could handle the year-long contract and the accompanying monthly bills. Just so long as I was careful and tried not to make many calls.

I was the first of the writing team to get a mobile and my colleagues roundly mocked me for it. Within an hour of owning it, they had arranged for someone to send me my first ever text message:

MR GORMAN. WE HAVE COMPLETED
YOUR SPERM COUNT
RESULT: ZERO

How we laughed.

They wouldn't have been there to witness the arrival of said text if it hadn't been the first day of my mobile phone-owning life. That day it was on because it was a novelty ... but it soon became my habit to turn the thing off when I got to the office and turn it on again when I left later that day. That wasn't just to protect myself from rogue 'sperm count' text messages; I didn't want to be disturbed when I was at work. A mobile phone was supposed to be a convenience but there was no point being silly with it. I didn't want people to be able to contact me whenever *they* wanted!

*

It is obvious that my nephews, nieces and – if I can put my laptop down for long enough to make any – my children will not remember these things in the same way. Their first email won't stick in their minds forever just as I have no recollection of writing my first letter or making my first phone call. Both were no doubt hugely exciting to me at the time but there's a big difference between taking a new step in the world you've always known and taking a leap into a whole, new, different and previously unimagined world.

But that new, different and previously unimagined world is where we now reside. It is a world of multi-channel television, high-speed internet and omnipresent mobile telephony. It is a world of laptops and tablets, of mousepads and touchscreens.

And it is a world of short attention spans. Why stay watching a YouTube video that hasn't grabbed your attention in the first ten seconds? The screen is full of links to others that might do better. Watching TV? Every ad break is an opportunity to see if there's something better on the other side. Or another, other side. Or another, other, other side. Or maybe to just scroll through the channels until you get lost and can't remember what you were watching in the first place.

But how much of the sensory bombardment do we really take in? I've spent the best part of today staring at various screens but the only things I can recall with any clarity are an odd video in which former Monkee Davy Jones discusses the Vietnam War with Noel Edmonds before singing a song on a set dressed to resemble a US army recruiting office,* another video in which a man uses a vacuum cleaner to give his daughter a perfect ponytail in just five seconds** and a long, bizarre and yet true story about a Hawaiian Mormon college football player of Samoan descent whose dead girlfriend turned out not to be dead at all ... because, um, she never actually existed.***

I know why those things have stayed in my mind but what about all the other information I've consumed today? Where did all *that* go? I mean, I also read a newspaper ... but not one part of it has lodged itself inside my brain.

On an average day, I think I must encounter a hundred

* http://gor.mn/DJnNoel
** http://gor.mn/vactail
*** http://gor.mn/GFhoax

times as much content as I did, say, ten years ago but it feels like I am retaining a hundred times less. Why? Is it all just disposable tat? Or is there just too much of it? So much that it's become impossible to deal with? If someone tosses three tennis balls your way, you'll probably catch at least one of them and maybe two ... but if instead they were to throw a hundred tennis balls at you, all at the same time, you'd duck for cover and catch none. And you'd probably emerge somewhat confused by the experience too. (Of course if someone filmed it and put it online you'd probably have some kind of viral hit on your hands.)

But what happens if you try and slow the world down and examine the maelstrom of data that's swirling about our heads? What happens if we look closely? If we don't just move on to the next thing and the next thing and the next thing? What happens if we think about it? If we consider what it is that surrounds us? Does it make sense? Or is it all just a load of balls?

CHAPTER 2

. . . .

WHAT'S NOT TO LIKE ABOUT MYLIKES?

There is too much information. The world is full of noise. The rising cacophony makes it hard for us to pick out only the tunes we want to hear. But we try. We try to shut out the unwanted information. We fast-forward through the ads. And just as we struggle to filter the wheat from the chaff ourselves, so we struggle to be heard. And so we shout louder. And so there is more noise. And so it goes on.

And on. And on. And on and on and on.

So we pay little attention to most of what passes before our eyes. We have trained our brains not to bother. But I think it is worth stopping sometimes and looking at it. *Really* looking at it. Because when you do, you finally see how little of it makes sense. You become aware of quite how much nonsense we have come to tacitly accept. We've built a ridiculous world for ourselves and we don't see it because we're no longer looking.

And on and on and on.

In this book I intend to address the things that clamour

for our attention. They fall into two broad categories. Those that confuse me and those that enrage me. Some of it is stuff that I simply cannot explain. Things that I do not pretend to understand.

Why, for example, when Michael Parkinson fronts a TV ad for life insurance, does the commercial start with him sitting in the dark? Why would he do that? There is no real-world situation where someone sits in the dark, alert and awake, waiting for the lights to come on before they speak. Well, I suppose it might happen if they're plotting a surprise birthday party for someone, but that's different.

But then there is the stuff that enrages me. These are things I *do* understand. Or at least I think I do. These are the things that – it seems to me – contribute nothing of value to our world. They serve no good. They benefit no one. These things add to the noise, but they are nothing but noise. These things are like litter that has been casually tossed aside by people who clearly couldn't care less about the rest of us. No. It is worse than litter. As much as I detest litter, at least it was once useful. At least that crisp packet you see fluttering in the gutter once contained crisps. It's not the crisp packet's fault it was so lazily discarded. But the virtual litter – the stuff that flutters around in the internet's gutter – never had any other purpose. It is as though someone is manufacturing empty crisp packets and distributing them straight to the gutter.

I suppose I should be up front and admit that I have been a virtual litterbug myself. Just the once, mind. It will only ever be the once.

On 4 December 2009 I tweeted the frankly vapid, '*I haven't been able to do this kind of mobile tweeting before. New phone – Motorola Dext – ends my luddite ways.*'

It is a conspicuously clunky sentence. Several years have passed since that tweet but its power to shame me lingers on. As I type this, I am blushing at the memory. Why would anyone mention the specific make and model of their phone in passing like that? It makes as much sense as, '*Thinking of having a cup of tea. Might put my Russell Hobbs kettle on in a minute.*' Ugh. What was I thinking?

Free phone! That's what I was thinking.

A PR company had contacted my agent to see if I wanted a Motorola Dext. It was mine if I wanted it, free of charge and with no obligation to do anything in return … only … well … '*it would be nice if, y'know, you could maybe mention it on Twitter or something? Y'know … only if you like it.*'

At the time I genuinely had no idea this sort of thing happened. I am not routinely offered freebies. I am neither a mover nor a shaker: this was something very much not-of-my-world. I weighed it up. On the one hand, my integrity was at stake. On the other hand … FREE PHONE! It was free! And it was a phone. I'm ashamed of myself, but I made my pact with the devil; I said yes. It won't happen again. I am wiser now. And I am sorry.

I became hyper-aware of other people tweeting about the phone in similarly gauche, brand-dropping ways. Every time I saw such a tweet it would make me feel momentarily better – sharing the sin made me feel like I carried less of the shame – and then I'd feel worse as I turned my judgement of others back on myself. Of course, I might have been wrong. For all I know the former England rugby captain, Will Carling, had bought his own phone and was tweeting the words, '*Trying out the new Motorola Dext – a little tricky at the mo, but will have a play!!*' in all innocence.[*]

If it's any consolation my phone didn't stand up to much use. Its keyboard soon developed a fault, making it pretty much unusable. I get the impression that Motorola weren't especially proud of it either. They certainly chose not to update its operating system meaning that it soon became incompatible with the majority of apps. It wasn't a very smart smartphone for long.

To be clear, it's not that I object to the idea of endorsing a product. I don't. I have no moral objection to advertising per se. It's the sense of dishonesty that grates.

A commercial on TV carries a lot of information with it just by dint of being a commercial. We watch ads with a vaguely cynical eye. We know why they exist. We know they're trying to play with our minds. We know they're there to persuade us to buy stuff. We know that the people

[*] http://gor.mn/MotDexWC

we see in them have been paid. We know all that before a word has been spoken. And knowing all that affects how much faith we put in what is said.

Does anyone think, for example, that Ant and Dec love Morrisons above all other supermarkets? They might do. But it seems a bit unlikely. I think most of us assume – rightly or wrongly – that their motivation for doing the ads was more financial than anything else. And once we've made *that* assumption, the assumption that they'd have been just as happy to recommend a rival supermarket naturally follows. Some people are quick to judge when a famous face appears in a commercial but whether you approve, disapprove or don't really give it that much thought, at least the arrangement has a degree of transparency about it: *you watched someone say some words that you know they were paid to say.*

Personally, I don't mind an honest liar. It's the dishonest ones I have a problem with. If I watch a magician perform a trick – for sake of argument, let's say, holding up a spoon that appears to bend of its own accord – I am entertained. But if the *same* performer was to do the same trick while *denying* that he was a magician then my entertainment would be somewhat curtailed. I can admire someone's sleight of hand, but I will resent his attempts to con me. Not that I know anyone who actually does that with spoons, you understand, that was just an example plucked from the ether at random.

When we read someone's tweets we assume we are

reading their uncensored – and unsolicited – words. Twitter is really just a conversation and it's disconcerting to think that people would be pretending to idly chat while slyly serving Mammon. If you're in the pub and a friend recommends a new band that they've heard on the radio, you assume that they're just genuinely enthused by the band's music, don't you? How would you feel if you later discover that a record company had paid them to casually drop the band into conversation every now and then? I think I'd feel more than a little let down. What kind of friend would do that?

Bearing all of that in mind, imagine my shock at receiving an email from a company called MyLikes. MyLikes weren't offering me a free phone in return for a tweet. They were offering me money. With MyLikes anyone can get paid for tweeting adverts.

Hi Dave!

I hope you are doing well. My name is Alex and I am a Community Manager with MyLikes. I'm reaching out to you because I think @DaveGorman is an account with lots of potential and an impressive number of followers. I noticed you aren't using our platform. I want to change this! We are the largest advertising platform on the social web, and we help publishers make the most of their tweets and make serious money.

That's right. MyLikes weren't offering me a free phone in return for a tweet. They were offering me money. The email continues:

> We do not make you spam your followers, we provide
> relevant content that your followers will love.

Yes. With MyLikes, anyone can get paid for tweeting adverts. But it's not spam. No. It's not spam. You got that? Not. Spam.

Hmmm.

I'm pretty sure it is spam, you know. It really is.

Alex's email went on to explain a little of how it works. Essentially, once you've signed up to the, um, 'platform' you can then choose between various, er, 'campaigns'. If you like the look of one, you simply click on a link and it automatically sends out a tweet from your account. The tweet contains a link and their systems measure how many times that link is clicked. The more people you can persuade to click on a link, the more money you get paid.

Alex's email contained various examples of the sort of links I could choose to share with the world. I think the idea here was to demonstrate that because this was exactly the sort of thing I was already sharing, nobody would think it at all odd and so nobody would notice that it was advertising. It would be advertising in disguise.

Alex's list of example links was truly remarkable. It was as if it had been compiled by someone who'd researched my personality, analysed my biometric data and studied the patterns of my online behaviour ... and then used all that insight to select the things I would be most likely to hate.

The chances of me – an Englishman with zero interest in American football – tweeting a link to an article titled 'We Rank The Dirtiest Players In The NFL' are slim at best. 'Hey everyone, here's a web page containing photos of men I've never heard of, playing a foreign sport I don't follow ... take a look!' No. I can't see it somehow.

Even less likely was the suggested 'The 15 Most "Bro" Colleges' article. My grasp of youthful American slang terms isn't great but I think 'The 15 Most "Bro" Colleges' probably translates as 'The 15 American Universities Most Populated With Obnoxious Dicks Who Brag About How Much They Drink And Call Each Other "Dude"', although I can't be sure.

There is barely a sentence in the piece that doesn't hurt my eyes in some way. Viz:

#15 University of Alabama:
Ranked in the Top 3 as one of the 'Best Colleges For Preppies', Alabama takes the inaugural crown for having bros that are tremendously stuck-up.

I've read that a dozen times and I still don't really know what it means. I'm pretty sure I understand the *individual* words, it's just that when they're put together in that order it sort of runs out of meaning. It involves measuring three qualities – bro-ness, preppy-ness and stuck-up-ness – that are, of course, immeasurable. But somehow the author has decided that the University of Alabama is fifteenth for bro-ness, on account of being third for preppy-ness, which of course puts it first for stuck-up-ness. What? It's a Russian doll of a sentence, where each layer makes less sense than the last. If I was to tweet a link to that kind of gibberish I don't think anyone would suspect I was being paid for it ... but I'm sure there'd be a few people wondering if I'd taken a knock to the head. And a few more hoping to deliver me one.

You can probably tell that I find the whole idea of MyLikes repellent, but I can't stop myself from being grimly fascinated by it too. As much as I wish it just didn't exist, I can't stop myself from wanting to know more about it. And so, like a child with the measles who can't resist picking at the spots, I find myself browsing their website. I know it's going to make it worse, but I have to look, I have to.

It's open on a window behind these words as I type them. If the site is to be believed, then their list of advertisers includes Nestlé, CBS, Samsung and 1-800-flowers.com. But I want to know more. I want details. And it's hard to find out the details without signing up.

So I've signed up. I have an account. I'm now a MyLikes publisher. Except I haven't published anything and I never will. I feel like an intruder ... but I haven't had to pick a lock or break a window ... anyone can click through to these pages ... the pages that show me what campaigns are available. At the top of the pile I see a campaign for something – or someone – called César Castellanos.

It's a someone. César Castellanos is a Colombian preacher and the campaign on MyLikes is there to drive people to his Twitter account – @CesarCaste – presumably in the hope that they will then follow him.

The suggested wording – although you're free to play with this, just so long as you leave the meaning intact – is *'Receive daily inspiration by the pastor of one of the largest churches in the world, Cesar Castellanos. <...link...]'*

As a MyLikes publisher, I can click on a button and post *that* message to Twitter. And if anyone reading my tweet then clicks on the link I will earn seven cents. Just think, if fifteen people click on it, I could make more than a dollar!

Am I the only person who feels a little uncomfortable about a pastor – a pastor from one of the largest churches in the world no less – paying people to increase his followers on Twitter? Surely someone with one of the largest churches in the world should have a willing army of followers, wanting to spread the word for more wholesome reasons than the potential to make fifty bucks if they can persuade 715 people to click on a link?

When I look at @CesarCaste I can see that Señor Castellanos has nearly 44,000 followers. How many of them followed him because they saw one of those tweets is unknowable, but I doubt there are many. Most of his own tweets are in Spanish. Most of his followers seem to be Spanish speakers too. The wisdom of tweeting English language ads for a Spanish-language account is hard to divine.

And I'm not convinced that the majority of people I can see tweeting the message '*Receive daily inspiration by the pastor of one of the largest churches in the world, Cesar Castellanos*' are doing so because they actually think their followers *should* receive that daily inspiration. Certainly I have yet to see those words tweeted by an account that is actually following Señor Castellanos.

At the top of the pile is an account called @SexCuriosities. Their other tweets say things like '*Dancing, singing and masturbating are all proven ways to fight depression*' and '*If days of the week were sex acts, Monday would be a dry, passionless handjob*'. There's no direct contradiction between these tweets and a call to prayer, but it does seem a little odd. It's hard to imagine many people follow them both … and sadly it's now going to be impossible to find out because while I was looking at the @SexCuriosities account it disappeared. One minute it was there, the next it was gone, deleted, kaput. I wonder what else they were up to?

So instead let's look at one of the other accounts that's tweeted on behalf of César Castellanos: @FootyGossip247. Pretty much all of their other tweets are – as you'd expect – about football. Mostly English football. The sentence '*Receive daily inspiration by the pastor of one of the largest churches in the world, Cesar Castellanos*' looks even odder when it immediately follows *'Millwall have signed mid-fielder Shaun Derry on a one-month loan deal from Queens Park Rangers'*.

I tweeted @FootyGossip247 to ask why they'd recommended following a man they don't bother to follow themselves. But they didn't reply. And nor did anyone else that I asked – most of which were fan-accounts, named in honour of various pop stars; Justin Bieber, Selena Gomez, the various members of One Direction ... you get the idea. In the end I asked more than two dozen people to explain why they'd tweeted this particular recommendation and not one of them replied. But then not one of them seems to use Twitter for any kind of conversation with anyone. Most of them tweet nothing but these kind of links.

I also asked @CesarCaste if he could tell me how much money had been spent on the campaign and if he knew how effective it had been ... but predictably enough he too didn't reply.

MyLikes sells itself as a place where ordinary people can use their Twitter accounts to earn a few bucks by linking to content that's exactly the sort of thing they'd have linked to anyway. And I'm sure there must be examples out there where this has happened. But I can't find one. I've looked at dozens of the different campaigns offered by MyLikes and each time, when I search Twitter to see who is actually tweeting the links, I just see the same pattern at work.

I looked at dozens of campaigns besides César Castellanos. There was a campaign for the foot-fetish website, ToeSuckingFun.com, and one for a Floridian air-conditioning company, Zippy Air Conditioning. There was a campaign to promote a Canadian band called Terrain and another to promote CrabRevenge.com – a website that sells pubic lice. (I wish I was making this up but sadly I'm not.) And there were many, many more.

In each case I'd look up the suggested wording for the ad and then search Twitter to see who – if anyone – had tweeted those words, and every time I would find pretty much the same thing.

There were two sorts of accounts involved. The first were themed accounts – accounts that tweet on one subject, whether it's sex, sport, a celebrity, horoscopes, recipes or whatever. When you see one of those accounts tweeting a link to a MyLikes campaign, it really stands out as it always seems to be a peculiarly odd break from the theme.

The second category is harder to define. They are small accounts. They often describe themselves as 'internet marketers'. They are normally being followed by a handful of similar accounts. Because nobody in their right mind wants to follow an internet marketer. And they do nothing but tweet things that they think will make them money. And because nobody real appears to be following them they can't get many clicks. And so they can't make very much money.

Not that that's what it's about. The test of whether MyLikes is of value shouldn't be whether or not people have made money out of it. I'm sure they have. But how?

If you happened to be following @FootyGossip247 and you saw them tweet '*Receive daily inspiration by the pastor of one of the largest churches in the world, Cesar Castellanos <...link...]*' you wouldn't know it was an advert. The only sensible conclusion you could draw was that the person behind @FootyGossip247 was sincerely recommending @CesarCaste and that they themselves take daily inspiration from him. Your brain isn't given the chance to assess it for what it is. You don't immediately see that @FootyGossip247 is to @CesarCaste what Ant and Dec are to Morrisons. It isn't the honest lie of an advert. It is the dishonest lie of an advert in disguise. And that undermines a part of what makes the internet work.

The internet thrives on word of mouse. People who like something recommend it to others. Link and click, link and click, link and click.

Commerce destroys that. If we can't tell the difference between a message that says, '*I like this and think you might like it too,*' and one that says, '*I'm pretending to like this and suggesting you might like it too because I'll get paid if you so much as take a look at it,*' then we'll end up viewing it all with suspicion. It doesn't add anything to the conversation. But it does add to the noise. Yet more noise. More unwelcome noise.

buffering

▮▮▮▮▮▮▮▮▮▮▮▮▮▮▮

CHAPTER 3

. . . .

IF EVERYONE CHECKS THE INTERNET FOR EVERYTHING THEN WHAT HAPPENS WHEN THE INTERNET GETS IT WRONG?

We have never had more information at our fingertips. But it comes at a cost. Which is that we have never had more misinformation at our fingertips, either. In order to navigate this mish-mash of fact, rumour and nonsense we have to sharpen our instincts and fine-tune our bullshit-radars. I'm not convinced we're making a very good fist of it.

It's a tiresome fact of modern life that we must question *everything* we're told. And I mean *everything*. The internet used to represent the fringes of human knowledge. It was where the weirdos hung out. It had less authority. If you *really* wanted to know something you went to the library and checked in a proper book. But the pixels have edged nearer and nearer to the heart of life and now, when the author of a book wants to check a fact he goes to the internet. So when the internet gets things wrong we all do.

If you went to school in the first decade of the 21st century you might well have studied William Blake's poem, 'Two Sunflowers Move into the Yellow Room'.

The only problem is it wasn't actually written by William Blake. In fact it wasn't written until more than 150 years after he'd popped his clogs. The true author is Nancy Willard. The poem was included in her 1981 anthology, *A Visit to William Blake's Inn*.

It seems the original misattribution came in 2001 when some students added it to a website as part of a project called *Poetry As We See It*. In the project they defined various elements of poetry and illustrated each with an example or two. In this instance, the poem was used to illustrate the use of 'personification'. In the mistaken belief that Willard had merely edited an anthology of Blake's poems, they gave the credit to him.

The site they'd added it to is one that invites teachers to use it as an educational resource and so – with nobody picking up the original error – it was rapidly magnified, spreading by word of mouse across the world wide web.

Respected teaching websites were soon listing it as an example of Blake's work, some of which run by US state universities. Major publishers and even government inspectors have repeated the error. A 2009 Ofsted report into a small East Sussex primary school noted that 'writing poetry based on William Blake's "Sunflowers"' was helping the kids to make 'good gains in their cultural development'.

The man credited with spotting the error is called Thomas Pitchford. He's a school librarian from Hitchin and when he saw the poem attributed to Blake he immediately thought something was amiss. To his educated eyes it just didn't seem to be in Blake's style at all and it's his detective work that has unravelled the mystery.

It's tempting to wonder why nobody else had spotted it sooner. '*Surely,*' splutters the bluff brigadier, '*an English teacher should know the words of William Blake when they see it!*' But can we really expect every English teacher to be a true William Blake aficionado? The only lines of Blake that I can quote are '*Tyger Tyger, burning bright, / In the forests of the night*' from 'The Tyger' and '*I hate you, Butler,*' from *On the Buses*, and I've a feeling one of those is from the wrong Blake.

The truth is people simply believe what they see written down. Why would anyone think a major publishing house had got it wrong? Surely even a true fan of Blake's writing would assume he must have written something in a slightly different style rather than questioning the veracity of a respected university's website.

Who knows what piece of work will be misattributed next? Lord Byron's 'There Was A Young Girl From Nantucket'?

*

I suspect there is something about the magic of today's technology that subtly encourages us to suspend our critical thinking. There was a time when even the most sophisticated technology in one's home was something a keen amateur could understand. It's not so long ago that every young Boy Scout built a rudimentary crystal radio receiver. But now the word 'wireless' has changed its meaning and hardly any of us could open up our computers and truly understand what any of the components do. And we certainly can't fix them when they break.

For me – and for millions like me – using Wi-Fi is essentially an act of faith. I don't know how it works, I just know that it does. I *know* that it's science but it might just as well be magic for all I can wrap my head around it. And why would magic get things wrong? Information feels really facty on a screen these days.

*

You have almost certainly seen a text, a tweet, a Facebook status or an email that goes a little like this:

> This March will have 5 Saturdays, 5 Sundays and 5
> Mondays. This only happens every 823 years!!!!

Some of the details might be different. Instead of March it might be July and instead of a Saturday/Sunday/Monday sequence it might be a Wednesday/Thursday/Friday, but essentially it's the same thing.

It is, as you've no doubt guessed, a load of old tosh. And this particular piece of tosh has a fingerprint. We can trace each iteration of this baloney back to a single source. Because these phenomena always, always, always include the '*823 years*' part. Why 823? Where on earth did that come from? It's so spectacularly wrong and random a choice that there's simply no way two people came up with it independently.

This lie must have been told millions of times but, like Rasputin, it refuses to die. It just wanders aimlessly around the internet, bubbling to the surface every few months as new hordes trip over it and share it in an orgy of gullibility.

It takes the tiniest amount of thought – or indeed, no thought and a diary – to see that it's not true. So why do so many people just help it on its way?

Just think about any sequence of 31 days.

Count them out in rows of seven – one for every day of the week – and you're always going to have three left over. So, whichever three days fall on the 1st, 2nd and 3rd will *always* occur five times in the month.

If the 1st of the month is a Saturday, then the 8th, 15th, 22nd and 29th will be Saturdays too. If the 3rd of the month is a Monday, so the 10th, 17th, 24th and 31st will follow.

Seven out of twelve months contain 31 days and every one of them will always contain five examples of

a three-day sequence of one kind or another. So, far from being extraordinary, it's actually happening *most* months of the year!

The particular example given – a March having five Saturdays, Sundays and Mondays – occurred in 2014. But we only have to wait eleven years for it to happen again. That's not quite the 823 years advertised!

In fact, in the next 823 years that exact same pattern will occur 117 times! In 2025, 2031, 2036, 2042, 2053 ... and so on and so on.

If you don't believe me, just count them all off and come back to me in 2837. I'll be the smug 866-year-old in the corner saying, 'I told you so.'

Not that you need to break it down mathematically to know that ...

This March will have 5 Saturdays, 5 Sundays and 5 Mondays. This only happens every 823 years!!!!

... just isn't true. In your gut you know the calendar doesn't work like that. You know that every calendar date rotates through the days of the week, albeit a little haphazardly. You know that the first of January is sometimes a Sunday, sometimes a Monday, sometimes a Tuesday and so on. You know that your birthday has sometimes fallen on the weekend and sometimes it hasn't. If someone told you that your birthday was a Wednesday this year and wouldn't be a Wednesday again for another 823 years you'd instantly see it for the lie that it is. And so the same must be true for *every* other day of the year.

And yet *something* makes people believe this. Something makes people forward it on. What?

I guess we all know that a month is *'about four weeks long'*. If you don't stop and think about it, I suppose that makes the presence of five Saturdays *sound* odd. *'There must be a rip in the space-time continuum,'* you think, *'because the calendar is definitely squeezing a quart into a pint pot there!'* And odd must be rare, because if it was common it wouldn't be odd. And I suppose it does remind you of that time on 11 December 2013 when everyone got really excited about the date being 11/12/13 and told each other that it was significant because it wouldn't be sequential like that for another 89 years and 52 days (unless you were American in which case a} your 11/12/13 had been about a month earlier and b} your 12/13/14 wasn't really all that far away).

And 89 years and 52 days is *nearly* 90 years and 90 years is *nearly* 100 years and 100 years is longer than you've got left and so that's really the same as 823 years when you think about it so, y'know, it's a bit like *that*, isn't it?

And so somehow you allow your brain to short circuit. You don't bother to question it. Because it's a seductive 'fact'. It's the kind of 'fact' that makes the world feel a bit more magical. Unlike those boring facty-facts that make the world seem a bit more prosaic. And why would *you* bother to check it anyway? I mean, your friend forwarded it on and they're trustworthy, aren't they? They probably checked it. Not that they'd need to. They're good with numbers. They love a sudoku.

But most importantly, this 'fact' travelled through thin air to your laptop and how else could it have done *that* if it wasn't flying along on gusts of hot truth, huh?

And so on it goes, for ever and ever and ever.[*] Mouseclick, mouseclick, rah rah blah.

*

Much was written as our calendars turned from 1999 to 2000. A huge Y2K industry sprung up out of nowhere. We waited for the Millennium Bug to strike. We expected planes to fall out of the sky and our bank accounts to evaporate … but it didn't happen.

---

[*] If you don't believe me – wait until there's a 31-day month starting and search Twitter for '823 years'. It's always there. In droves.

But it wasn't the year 2000 we should have been scared of. It was the years 2001 to 2013 that were the problem. And it wasn't the computers that were going to break down, it was us. With twelve months in a year, the first twelve-plus-one years on the meter were the ones that provided the most of *those* dates. We've had 01/01/01, and 02/02/02, and 03/03/03 right through to 12/12/12. We've had patterns and sequences and palindromes aplenty and each and every time the world has gone bat-shit crazy.

On 12 December 2012, I was in a queue – waiting to buy some mince pies if you must know – and I genuinely overheard a young couple having the following conversation:

Him: *Y'know it's 12/12/12 today, dontcha?*
Her: *Is it?*
Him: *Yeah, I saw it on Facebook.*

The hint that the date would have been an unknowable fact for them without the presence of Facebook is already remarkable. But it got worse. Because he went on to say what must have been the single most ridiculous sentence I'd ever heard:

Him: *It's a good job there aren't thirteen months or imagine how unlucky 13/13/13 would be this time next year!*

Just take that in. How do you begin to process a sentence like that?

'*It's a good job …*'

Yes. Yes. I think we can all agree that we dodged a bullet on that one, didn't we? I'm so glad the referendum went the way it did and we settled on the old twelve months in a year and not thirteen, aren't you?

'*Imagine …*'

Are you imagining it? It's tricky, isn't it? You have to forget the fact that *if* we had thirteen months in a year, *that* particular day wouldn't have been the twelfth of the twelfth of the twelfth anyway.

And you have to forget the fact that, even if it *had* been, '*this time next year*' would obviously be the twelfth of the twelfth of the thirteenth and not the thirteenth of the thirteenth of the thirteenth.

So forget all that. And just try to imagine how unlucky the thirteenth of the thirteenth of the thirteenth would be. It's hard, isn't it? Because it would be the thirteenth of the thirteenth of the thirteenth *all* day, *everywhere*. For everyone. Nobody would have any good luck. Everyone would have bad luck. Everyone. That's almost too much bad luck to contemplate.

Their little exchange had set my head spinning. But it wasn't over yet. Because the record for 'single most ridiculous sentence I'd ever heard' was about to be snatched away from his hands. So soon! It turned out she was more able than I to contemplate just how unlucky that mythical day would be. The very thought of it made her shudder. And then her eyes widened. A new thought had landed. She turned to her man, rolled her eyes and said, '*Ooh ... knowing us, I bet it'd be a bloody Friday as well!*'

CHAPTER 4

• • • • • • • • • • • •

WHATEVER YOU DO, DON'T LOOK THE
DAILY EXPRESS IN THE EYE

Newspapers have habits. Each title has its little quirks. Nowhere is this more clearly demonstrated than on the front page of the *Daily Express*. I don't think any other paper displays quite such a narrow focus.

The Duchess of Cornwall, Princess Diana, Madeleine McCann, immigrants, house prices and magical medical cures are pretty much the only things on their agenda.

In the first six months of 2013 Kate Windsor née Middleton graced the cover 26 times. That's fourteen per cent of their available covers!

In the same time frame, eleven of the headlines were about a rise in house prices:

February 7th: **HOUSE PRICES ON RISE AGAIN**

March 2nd: **HOUSE PRICES ARE UP AGAIN**

March 18th: **HOUSE PRICES UP £142 A DAY**

April 1st: **HOUSE PRICES SET TO SOAR**

April 26th: **HOUSE PRICES TO RISE BY £10,000**

May 7th: **HOUSE PRICES TO SOAR BY 30%**

May 20th:	**HOUSE PRICES AT RECORD HIGH**
May 31st:	**HOUSE PRICES SURGE AGAIN**
June 14th:	**RECORD HIGH FOR HOUSE PRICES**
June 19th:	**HOUSE PRICES RISE BY £9,000**
June 29th:	**HOUSE PRICES KEEP RISING**

When you see them laid out like that – and especially when you see how tightly bunched some of them are – it's hard not to characterise the newspaper as one of those mad men you sometimes see at the bus stop. You know the one I mean: he won't stop repeating himself until someone – anyone – acknowledges his existence despite the fact that he's only got one thing to say.

'I see house prices are on the rise again.'

You look at your feet and pretend you haven't heard him.

'Did you hear me?' he says. 'I said, house prices are up again.'

You check your phone, hoping against hope that there'll be a new text message that deserves your full attention.

'£142 a day, I reckon.'

You *want* to look up. You want to see if he *looks* as crazy as he sounds. But if you do, you might make eye contact. You can't make eye contact. He'll reel you in if you make eye contact.

'Soar, I tell you,' he continues. 'They're going to soar. House prices, I mean. I reckon we could be looking at thirty grand!'

You can't resist sneaking a peek. Against your better judgement you look up. He catches your eye.

'I'll tell you what.' He leans in. 'That Princess Kate, she's a bit of all right, isn't she? Phwoar!'

What does it mean anyway? If house prices have risen by ten grand in April and nine grand in June, have they risen by nineteen grand in total? Or is the June headline telling us they were one grand out in April?

I think what it really means is that the *Express* have done some research that reveals they sell more copies whenever they run that headline – and let's be honest, it is pretty much one headline – and as a result someone has been tasked with the job of scouring every survey by every mortgage broker and finding the best way to spin it.

But the *Express* really comes into its own when it comes to the 'miracle cure' story. In the first six months of 2013, more than one in four of the *Daily Express*'s front pages carried this kind of story. More than one in four!

The first one came on 7 January with the headline **'SUPER PILL IS KEY TO LIVING LONGER'**. It's a story about a pill that the paper gleefully tells us is 'made out of tomatoes' and which 'could hold the key to beating arthritis, diabetes, heart disease and even cancer'. It's funny how the word 'could' has crept into the story when the headline seemed so much more certain, isn't it?

It probably won't come as much of a surprise to you to learn that when the story quotes some of those connected to the research, their message feels a whole lot less certain.

'We think these results are good news and potentially very significant, but we need more trials to see if they translate into fewer heart attacks and strokes,' says one.

'It is too early to come to any firm conclusions,' says another.

And I can't help feeling that it probably would have been better if the *Express*'s headline writer had taken his advice. There's something about putting '**SUPER PILL IS KEY TO LIVING LONGER**' in massive lettering on the front of your paper that suggests a firm conclusion has been reached. Or jumped to.

Anyway, this early story is perfect for the *Express* as it addresses most of its favourite illnesses. By my reckoning, it only really needed to offer a cure for dementia to collect the set. Because while heart disease is up there, it's really arthritis, dementia, diabetes and cancer that dominate proceedings.

Allow me to try and demonstrate the full scale of the paper's approach by going through them one illness at a time.

Let's start with arthritis.

How's this for a sequence of front-page headlines:

January 21st: **SIMPLE TEST TO SPOT ARTHRITIS EARLY**

January 30th: **WONDER 'JELLY' THAT CAN HELP BEAT ARTHRITIS**

February 8th: **SINGLE JAB CAN BEAT ARTHRITIS**

February 16th: **NEW JAB TO FIGHT MISERY OF ARTHRITIS**

February 22nd: **ARTHRITIS: NEW BREAKTHROUGH**

March 14th:	**ARTHRITIS: NEW JAB TO FIGHT THE PAIN**
April 10th:	**GEL TO WIPE OUT ARTHRITIC PAIN**
May 6th:	**WONDER 'OIL' TO END ARTHRITIS AGONY**
May 28th:	**WONDER PILL CUTS RISK OF ARTHRITIS**
June 22nd:	**EARLY TEST TO BEAT ARTHRITIS**

Bear in mind that these are just the *front-page* stories – there were other similar stories that didn't make the cover – and these are all from just a six-month period of time! And in all but one of these cases, we're talking about the paper's lead story of the day: *the one thing* they thought was of most significance to their readers.

If you view it as a conversation with their readership it rapidly descends into farce. It's like an Abbott & Costello 'Who's on first base?'-style routine gone wrong.

Is the new jab to fight the pain they mention on 14 March the same as the new jab they mention on 16 February or is it a new, new jab? And is *that* new jab different to the single jab they mentioned on 8 February?

And what are we to make of the wonder 'oil' and the wonder 'jelly'? Why the inverted commas? If it's not an oil, what is it? If it's not a jelly, what is it? Is it a gel? If so, is it the gel they're going on about on 10 April? At least we know that the wonder pill is a real pill. And that early test to beat arthritis? Is that the same as the simple test to spot arthritis early that they mentioned earlier and if not, how simple is it? And in what order should one take the tests? Which test should be earlier? The early test that beats it or the simple one that spots it early? So many questions. So few answers.

If you subscribe to the *Express* and you don't find yourself screaming, '*Yes! I know! You've told me that already!*', then you might be the reason they spend so much time talking about dementia cures as well.

You might be the reason they spend so much time talking about dementia cures as well.

January 8th:	**HOW BLOOD PRESSURE DRUG BEATS DEMENTIA**
January 25th:	**THE PILL TO BEAT ALZHEIMER'S**
March 6th:	**3p BLOOD PRESSURE PILL BEATS DEMENTIA**
May 21st:	**HOW DAILY VITAMIN B PILL FIGHTS DEMENTIA**
June 5th:	**DEMENTIA PILL THAT CAN SAVE YOUR LIFE**

I imagine you're starting to see the pattern now. The *Express* wants us to believe in the magic bullet. That pill, jab, gel or jelly that will, like Lily The Pink's medicinal compound, solve all our problems in one hit. I suppose it's comforting reading. But I'm not convinced it's a particularly healthy way to approach the health of your readers.

Sometimes it feels as if the *Express* can't be bothered to actually find news. It's as if they've got the four or five headlines they need most ready to go and just shuffle a few nouns around. It's as if the editor's there late at night taking the word arthritis out and putting diabetes in instead – not because of the news agenda but because it's a better fit on the page now that they've chosen the next day's picture of Kate.

March 4th:	**NEW HOPE IN FIGHT AGAINST DIABETES**
April 19th:	**SIMPLE CHECK-UP TO BEAT DIABETES**
May 1st:	**NEW DAILY JAB BEATS DIABETES**
June 3rd:	**EXCITING DIABETES CURE ON THE WAY**
June 13th:	**REGULAR WALKING FIGHTS OFF DIABETES**

And I missed out the 16 March double whammy '**DIABETES PILL BEATS CANCER**' on the grounds that I think it's a more comfortable bedfellow with:

| March 30th: | **PROOF ASPIRIN FIGHTS CANCER** |
| May 3rd: | **STATINS SLASH RISK OF CANCER** |

and

| June 25th: | **PILL TO PREVENT BREAST CANCER** |

And by the way, if that 3 May headline – '**STATINS SLASH RISK OF CANCER**' – doesn't help me shine a light on the recklessness of this approach then I don't know what will.

So far I've only been counting the 'magical cure' stories. When I tell you that in a full six months, they ran a story of that ilk on the front page more than one in four times, that only includes the feel-good, maybe-we'll-live-forever stories. It doesn't include the feel-bad, we're-all-going-to-die stories. And there are a fair few of them too. And statins have provided both. And no matter which it is, the *Daily Express* seems to love statins.

On 8 April 2013 their lead story was **'PROOF STATINS SAVE YOUR LIFE'**. That 28 May wonder pill that cuts the risk of arthritis? Turns out that was all about statins too. And yet, on 20 March, their lead story was **'STATINS IN NEW HEALTH ALERT – DAILY PILL CAN CAUSE KIDNEY DAMAGE'**.

If you ever find yourself telling people something will kill them one day only to find yourself telling them it will save their life just nineteen days later and you don't come away thinking that maybe, just maybe, this is the kind of story that you ought to handle more cautiously in future, then I don't know that you're ever going to take the hint.

Still, Kate's looking lovely, isn't she? Have they run that picture before? I don't know. Just look at her bewitching smile. Aw. Isn't she lovely!

CHAPTER 5

• • • • • • • • • • • •

IF IT ISN'T ONE OF YOUR GREATEST HITS
DON'T PUT IT ON A GREATEST HITS ALBUM

I'm sitting in a hotel room in Cornwall. The walk from my hotel to the theatre where I'll be performing tonight will only take a couple of minutes but it is bucketing down with rain so I'm staying in my room a little longer than I should. I'm ready to go though. Just waiting; hoping the rain will stop for long enough to allow me to make the dash and stay dry. While I stare out of the window and wait, I'm listening to some music that I'm streaming through my laptop. For once we seem to have landed in a hotel where the Wi-Fi is not only free but working reliably. My phone beeps to tell me I have a text message. I assume it's my tour manager, Kumar. He'll be backstage already. He'll be wondering where I am. He'll be hoping I haven't fallen asleep. Or been kidnapped. I pick up my phone and take a look. It isn't from Kumar. It's from a friend, Bryn. It says, '*I can't believe you're listening to The Wombles! Grow up.*'

What? How the hell does Bryn know I'm listening to The Wombles? Bryn lives in Liverpool. He's over 200 miles away. The music wasn't on *that* loud. I doubt it was even on loud enough to be heard in the room next door. Not that it matters because I know Bryn's not in the room next door. I met the person from the room next door in the corridor earlier and they definitely weren't Bryn. Not unless he's disguised himself as a 70-year-old woman. Which would be weird. I suppose he could be in the room with her. Maybe he's having an illicit affair? It seems unlikely. And not just because she must be four decades older than him. An affair is the kind of thing most people want to keep secret. If he's trying to keep his presence in the room next door a secret, sending me a text message about my music selection is a dumb way to go about it.

So I text him back: '*How the hell do you know I'm listening to The Wombles?*'

It is a matter of seconds before he replies: '*Facebook.*'

Of course. Facebook is a grass. He must have seen one of those notifications: '*Dave Gorman was listening to Banana Rock by The Wombles on Spotify.*'

I hate those. Can't a man listen to The Wombles in a hotel room without being the subject of mockery from his friends?

Ever since Bryn's text message I have been afflicted by Facebook paranoia.

I know that when I see a Facebook notification saying something like '*Gary is reading an article about political corruption on the Guardian website*' it's supposed to make me think, '*Ooh ... maybe I'd be interested in the same article,*' but it doesn't. It just makes me think, '*Shit ... I hope Facebook isn't sharing my selection of online reading material with everyone I know because I'm going to look a right twonk if it is!*'

I mention all this, not because I want to discuss Facebook paranoia but because I think it helps explain quite why my eyes alighted on something else a few months later.

I was at home. I was in the front room, watching – but not really watching – some TV and I'd just picked up my laptop to check on something. I was logged into Facebook but I wasn't paying it any great attention and yet somehow, through the mass of information on that page, my brain singled out one fact: Bryn had liked a status update from the indie rock band, Scouting For Girls.

The band's message, posted on 4 June 2013, reads as follows:

> Our Greatest Hits album, 10 years in the making, is
> now available to pre-order right now and features 2
> brand new tracks, 'Millionaire' and 'Make That Girl
> Mine'.

Would it have leapt out at me if Bryn and I hadn't had our earlier exchange? Was I subconsciously looking out for anything on Facebook that would expose Bryn's musical tastes? I don't know. I only know that I saw it. And I know that as I read the band's update I thought Bryn was an idiot for liking it.

But I didn't send him a text message mocking him for it. I'm classier than that.

I sent him an email. I had to. I needed to go into detail. I'd created a graph to help me make my case and I wanted to send him that as an attachment. A text message simply wouldn't have covered it.

To be clear, it's not because I think Scouting For Girls are more risible than The Wombles – I doubt many people would concur and besides I've no time for any such musical snobbery. Nor is it to do with the strange *'now available to pre-order right now'* clause with its confusing blend of immediacy and, um, pre-immediacy. That's not my beef.

No. The band's status update was a perfect illustration of a problem far greater than the band itself. It's a problem that exists across the whole of the music industry. I take issue with greatest hits compilations.

I don't have a problem with the *concept* of them existing, you understand. I'm not one of those people who thinks that to truly respect an artist one must consume their music only in the context of the original releases.

It may well be that some musicians see each album as a document that defines their presence in the world at a particular time and place. They may well have sweated over the precise running order of the ten or eleven tracks on a CD, and it might be that they've managed to strike a surprising narrative arc or what have you ... but if tracks three and five don't float my boat and it turns out that I only really liked the singles, then that effort was wasted on me and I'm happy to enjoy the stuff that moves me in whatever order I like, thank you very much.

My problem isn't so much with the concept of a greatest hits album, but with the way in which it is so often realised. And the phrase within the Scouting For Girls status update that sums it all up is this: '*features 2 brand new tracks.*'

Oh, does it now? Two brand new, never-been-released-before tracks? How does that work then? I mean, if they haven't been released yet they can't be hits. And if they're not hits they can't be greatest hits. And isn't that what a greatest hits album is supposed to contain? The clue is in the words 'greatest hits'.

I don't have a particular axe to grind with Scouting For Girls, by the way. I know they're not the only culprits. But no matter who the artist, if you show me a greatest hits album that features 'two brand new tracks' I'll show you two brand new tracks that are destined not to be hits. Has any band *ever* had a hit with a new song from a greatest hits album? I don't think so.

But, while we're here, what were Scouting For Girls doing releasing a greatest hits album in 2013 anyway? Have they had a long enough career, peppered with sufficiently great hits, to justify such a thing? How can a band that's released just three studio albums – with a combined total of 31 songs – amass enough hits for a fifteen-track greatest hits compilation?

This has got nothing to do with whether or not I (or you) *like* the band. I'm not making qualitative judgements about their music; such things are a matter of taste. But whether or not a song is a hit is not a matter of taste. It is a matter of record.

What is the definition of a hit? I think we can all agree that if a song reaches the top ten it's *obviously* a hit. But what about songs that chart outside of that? What about the top 40? That seems fair enough to me. For some reason the music industry seems to have settled on the 'top 40' as the standard. I don't know why it's not the top 50, 60 or any other number for that matter, I only know that across the world, in different markets, a top 40 chart countdown has become commonplace. And if that's the case, it seems reasonable to me to define anything that makes the top 40 a hit, and anything that doesn't, um, not-a-hit.

If that's the definition, how do Scouting For Girls stack up for hits?

Prior to the greatest hits compilation, they had released three studio albums. Their first album, also called *Scouting For Girls*, in 2007, their second, *Everybody Wants To Be On TV*, in 2010 and their third, *The Light Between Us*, in 2012.

Each album spawned a number of singles and the strategy appears to have been as follows: *keep releasing singles until one fails, then go to work on the next album. Rinse and repeat.* But with each album the point of failure has arrived sooner. So while the first album spawned six singles, viz:

Album 1: *Scouting For Girls*

Title	UK Singles Chart Position
She's So Lovely	7
Elvis Ain't Dead	8
Heartbeat	10
It's Not About You	38
I Wish I Was James Bond	40
Keep On Walking	198

… the second and third albums yielded four and then three:

Album 2: *Everybody Wants To Be On TV*

Title	UK Singles Chart Position
This Ain't A Love Song	1
Famous	37
Don't Want To Leave You	69
Take A Chance	Did not chart

Album 3: *The Light Between Us*

Title	UK Singles Chart Position
Love How It Hurts	17
Summertime In The City	73
Without You	Did not chart

It was this data I'd illustrated in graph form for Bryn's edification. I wanted him to see the pattern: it clearly shows that the rate of decline was getting steeper with each album the band released:

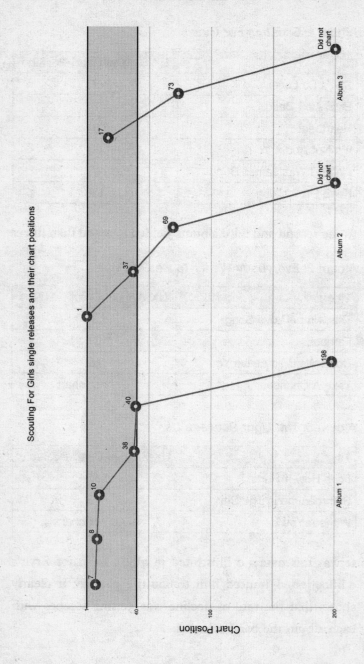

Scouting For Girls single releases and their chart positions

Chart Position

By my reckoning that's thirteen singles, of which only eight are bona fide 'hits' (and three of those are pushing it). Of the rest, two are a bit disappointing and three could probably be airbrushed out of history without anyone really noticing.

And yet *all thirteen* of these singles appear on the greatest hits album alongside the two new songs. How can the words 'greatest hits' be used to describe one song that got to number 198, two that didn't chart at all and two that the public haven't yet voted on? You might well think they're great, but they don't meet any definition of 'hit'. Wouldn't a more realistic title for the album be *Every Single We've Ever Released Plus The Two New Ones We Haven't?* I know it's not as catchy, but at least it would be honest.

I haven't listened to the album. For all I know they could be fantastic songs. Chart success is no measure of musical virtue, after all. It's certainly true that many of my favourite songs will never trouble the charts. But a hit is a hit is a hit and a song that barely scrapes into the top 200 isn't one.

But this isn't just a pedantic, semantic argument. If the album had instead been named *The Best Of ...*, making it a qualitative statement, a matter of opinion, no more, no less, my objection to the two new songs being there would remain.

Who, one wonders, is this album aimed at? It seems to me that there are two sorts of people likely to buy the Scouting For Girls *Greatest Hits* CD.

First there will be the casual listener who picks up the CD in a shop somewhere and thinks, *'Blimey, I didn't know they'd had fifteen hits! Still, if they're all as toe-tappy as the couple I can remember it can't be too bad ... after all, a hit is a hit. At least this way I'm not paying for any of those filler tracks you get on a regular album. I hate it when bands do that!'*

They'll think it's a safe bet. But then, four tracks in, they'll find themselves thinking, *'Hang on ... I don't remember hearing this one on the radio,'* and the doubt will start to creep in. By the time they're done they'll have come to the conclusion that at least five of the tracks were precisely the kind of filler they were hoping to avoid.

The second type of consumer is the Scouting For Girls super-fan. The fan who wants *everything* they do. This person has already bought the three existing albums. They already own the first thirteen songs – the hits, the not-quite-hits and the definitely-not-hits – but they want the two new songs. They want to show their support for the band. They want to slide the CD on to the shelf next to the others because the idea of their collection being incomplete pains them in some way.

So effectively, pretty much everyone is being conned. You want the hits? You've got to pay for the five non-hits and the two mystery songs too. You want the two new songs? Sure, just spin past the thirteen songs you already own first. Thanks for buying them again though. Kerching.

POSTSCRIPT

When I showed my wife, Beth, the email I'd sent to Bryn she was appalled. My plea for clemency – '*But he mocked me for liking The Wombles!*'– didn't go down very well. 'He had a bloody point,' she said. 'You're a grown man.'

That said, Bryn and I remain friends and I think he found my words persuasive. At least he decided to 'unlike' that particular status update and I think that has to count for something.

Bryn's birthday falls in July and Beth insisted on me sending him a present with a note of apology 'for being a stroppy git'. Bryn says he likes the present very much but that he never really listens to the two new tracks on the end. QED.

Chapter 6

· · · · · · · · · · · ·

'MUSIC FROM & INSPIRED BY THE MOTION PICTURE' CAN SOD OFF TOO

While I'm sorting out what tracks do or do not belong on a greatest hits album, I might as well address another musical bugbear of mine at the same time.

If it's your job to compile movie soundtrack albums, can you please try applying the following test first:

Was this song in the film?

Yes ☐ Stick it on the album.

No ☐ Leave it off the album. Don't include it using the feeble excuse that it was 'inspired by' the movie. It wasn't. You know it. And you know that we know it. And you know that we know you know we know it. 'Music from and inspired by the film *Smurfs 2*' is a ridiculous sentence. Nothing – no music, no any-thing – has ever been inspired by the film *Smurfs 2* and you're only making yourself look silly by pre-tending that it was.

Chapter 7

. . . .

SOME THINGS CAN BE PUT TO A PUBLIC VOTE … AND SOME THINGS REALLY CAN'T

It's easy to be cynical when a big corporation makes a big donation to a charity. When the CEO of Big Supermarket Inc. turns up during the peak-viewing hour of a major telethon, wielding one of those huge, oversized cheques '*on behalf of all our customers and staff*', it's easy to say that they're only doing it for the publicity. Personally, I doubt it's ever *only* for that reason. Of course it's *a part of the reason* – but I just can't bring myself to get worked up about it. After all, doing something good is probably a better way of generating publicity than, y'know, just paying for publicity and it's not as if they don't do plenty of that too. The charity involved is obviously delighted, nobody seems to be losing out as a result and so as far as I'm concerned my knickers remain untwisted.

But social media has changed things. Companies have become obsessed with the idea of generating a buzz online. They want to trend on Twitter. They crave

Facebook likes. And if their charitable works can be used to help drive such things, so much the better.

Or so much the worse.

Because lately I've been finding myself deeply offended by the way in which certain companies are turning their charitable donations into prizes that charities must compete for. Yes. You did read that correctly.

If you use Twitter you will almost certainly have seen a heartbreaking tweet that looks something like this: '*Please click here & vote! Your vote can help this little girl raise the money for an operation that will help her walk again!*'

How can you resist? It's not *even* asking for money! Just a vote! Someone else is going to donate money if you vote? It's a no-brainer. So you click. And you get taken to a page explaining that a company has £10,000 to donate to one of ten good causes and that the money will go to whichever one gets the most votes.

And all of a sudden, it's not as simple as a vote *for* a little girl in need of an operation. It's also, effectively, a vote *against* nine other *equally* deserving good causes. How dare they?!

There are ten good causes all lined up on the page. But only one of them will receive the £10,000. It's like a weird, twisted, screwed-up, dystopian version of *The X Factor* where they've given up on singing and it's now just the sadness of one's plight that counts. I can't in good conscience vote for any of them because I simply can't bring myself to vote *against* any of them and I deeply resent being asked to do so.

The mechanics of this competition appear to me to be pretty bloody transparent and ugly at the core.

Imagine you are raising money in the hope of transforming – or even saving – the life of your child, your parent or your spouse. Now imagine there is an opportunity to win £10,000. All you have to do is tell this company about your cause and hope that you're selected for the competition. They do select you. Now *all* you have to do is get the most votes.

Under those circumstances what else are you going to do but campaign hard? Of course you're going to mount a Facebook campaign and petition your friends. Of course you're going to tweet, tweet, tweet till your fingers bleed. Nothing will stop you. And nor should it.

But everyone involved with the other causes is just as keenly motivated. The company has effectively unleashed an army of PR foot soldiers, each one of them encouraging others to sign up to the cause.

'Don't just vote. Please RT.'

'We really need all the help we can get here, guys.'

'Just one more push. Please help.'

So everyone is pushing. And what they're pushing is a link to a page, emblazoned with the company's logo and boasting of its largesse. The company obviously thinks this is a brilliant ruse. How many hits do they get? Forty thousand? Fifty thousand? A hundred thousand? And all for just a ten grand outlay? And everyone who looks at the page sees how nice they are with their big donation to charity! Fantastic!

But what about the day after the votes have been counted? How do the people who were committed to the non-prize-winning causes feel then? *'I'm sorry, your disease will have to remain untreated ... not enough people voted for you. You should have campaigned harder. You should have had a more photogenic child. You should have looked sadder.'*

Isn't that just a little bit obscene? Isn't that just a tad grotesque? How dare they put people in that position. Why can't they exercise *their* own conscience, pick the cause *they* want to support and then just back it?

It's not even as though it's a real vote. Not in any meaningful way. How many people go to the website because they are aware of the competition and want to assess *all the available options* and weigh up which is the most worthy? Never have I seen a tweet that says, *'There are ten good causes here, please help us decide which one gets our support.'* It is only ever partisan links that lead you to these pages.

It's the same with pretty much all online votes.

Here are ten short films from new film-makers – but which one is going to win a grant?

Here are three great new tracks from three unsigned bands – but which one is going to get some airplay?

Here are fifteen models who want to be in our next ad campaign – but which one should we use?

Votes like these aren't decided by neutral observers who've weighed up all of the candidates and then voted with their heads and their hearts. They're won by whichever one of the interested parties is best at rallying support.

And that might be fine when we're talking about playing a single on the radio, but it seems pretty brutal and unpleasant when we're talking about a matter of conscience; about people in desperate need of funds, whose lives are being torn apart by crises and whose emotions are, one assumes, already on the rack. How must it feel to come a close second in a race of that kind?

It is impossible for any of us to actually measure how deserving *all* of the charities in the world are. How could one begin to calibrate such a thing?

Let's say you have a sum of money available to give to a charity. It could be ten pounds, a hundred pounds, a thousand or more, it doesn't matter; it's whatever you can afford and are willing to donate. How many hundreds of thousands of good causes *could* you donate it to? How could you begin to rank them in order of deservingness? It's not possible. You can't. And so you don't. That's not how you decide to divvy up your good deeds. It's simply not how it works.

When you sponsor a friend who's running a half marathon you do it because it's a good cause and you're a supportive friend. You don't do it because you've assessed every charity in the world and decided this is *the* best way to spend your charity-dollar. If a stranger had approached you and asked you to sponsor them for the same run, you *probably* wouldn't have done so.

Sometimes you feel moved to fundraise yourself. Sometimes your friends and colleagues do and you sponsor them. Sometimes the extraordinary efforts of an extraordinary stranger will persuade you to dip into your pocket. An advert, a leaflet, a mailshot, a news story, a collecting tin ... these are all these things can tug at your conscience and persuade you at different times. But what would happen in those moments if, instead of opening your wallet, you paused for thought and tried to weigh up whether or not there was a better, more deserving cause? Would you end up making wiser choices? I suspect you would just make *fewer* choices. Wouldn't we all just be paralysed by guilt? Would any of us be able to decide?

But that, in a microcosm, is what these public votes ask us to do. '*Which one of these people most deserves our help?*' they ask. How dare the companies behind these schemes absolve themselves of this responsibility! How dare they force us into this impossible position? They should do what everyone else does: pick a cause that touches *their* hearts and bloody well back it.

Not everything can be a competition. Not everything is about how many hits you can get on your website. What if the most deserving cause doesn't have a Twitter account? What happens then?

CHAPTER 8

. . . .

I KNOW THEY MAKE MAKE-UP BUT I WONDER HOW THEY MAKE UP THE THINGS THEY SAY THEIR MAKE-UP CAN DO?

When it comes to household chores I find most couples know each other's strengths and weaknesses pretty well. It's certainly true in the Gorman household. There's no debate about it, we both cheerfully acknowledge that Beth is a far better cook than me and I'm far handier with a drill. I apologise for conforming to gender stereotypes. If it helps, Beth's better with a tin of paint and a roller, and I'm the one who sews on any missing buttons.

But there is one task we can't agree on. There is one thing that we're both convinced we do better than the other: fast forwarding the TV through the commercial breaks.

When there's a drama we both like we *have* to watch it together. It just wouldn't do if one of us knew who the murderer was before the other. Watching an episode alone would be tantamount to infidelity. And because we keep unconventional hours we end up recording a lot of TV, sometimes bingeing on three or four hours' worth of a show in one sitting to bring ourselves up to date. Even when the fates conspire to mean we are both in at the right time to watch a show when broadcast, we'll often pause the TV for ten minutes at the start because that means we'll be able to fast forward through the ads later.

The ability to pause, rewind and fast forward TV is one of the ultimate joys of modern life. On our system you can go up to thirty times faster than normal. If you press the >> button once it will go twice as fast. Press it again and it goes up to six times the speed. Then twelve. Then thirty.

Two and six are relatively easy to control. Twelve is tricky. Only an expert with ninja-like reactions can cope with thirty. That car manufacturers routinely produce family saloon cars with top speeds in excess of 130 mph seems like an act of madness to me and I feel much the same about a remote control that goes at thirty times the speed of television. Is it really something you want just anybody to get their mitts on? Isn't there some kind of Advanced Remote Control test they should pass first? If you're viewing at 30x it only takes a split second of indecision and you find yourself watching a show from a minute or two in. Spoilers ahoy. It's a disaster waiting to happen.

Anyway, Beth thinks she's the most gifted fast-forwarder in our household. She's wrong. I am. She thinks she can cope with 30x. She's wrong. Only I can. (I can prove this using the IMB principle.)*

We were watching a *Poirot* one time and Beth insisted on being in charge of the remote. I knew it was a bad idea. She'd had a glass of wine. I don't normally approve of drinking-and-remoting but on this occasion my hands were full so she had to do it. I'd been tricked. Beth had asked me to sew a button on to a blouse she wanted to wear to work the next day. Once I'd started sewing, I couldn't really abandon it for an ad break now, could I?

Needless to say she sailed right through the ads and into a scene set in a railway station. We heard a couple of lines of dialogue that we shouldn't have before old muddle-thumbs got the thing back in gear and started to rewind. Instead of edging backwards at a sedate 6x, she instead tried to go for 30x in reverse and overshot the other way, landing us halfway back into the ad break we'd been trying to avoid in the first place. She muttered something unconvincing about how the batteries must be playing up and then went too far forward and backwards another two times before eventually hitting pause.

I looked up to see the final frame of the final ad frozen on the screen before me. It was an ad I'd seen before. But it was an ad I'd never paid any attention to before. It was advertising a foundation called Match Perfection from the make-up brand Rimmel. There was some small print

* It's My Book.

written in white text at the foot of the screen. When it's whizzing by at speed you obviously don't take it in but now that it was a freeze-frame I could read it clearly.

71% of 99 women agree.

I had no idea what it related to at that moment … but it didn't really matter. As stats go, isn't it just a little bit ridiculous? This ad must have cost hundreds of thousands of pounds and yet they were basing their claims on a survey of just *99* women! Would the budget not stretch to asking just one more woman? They're spending all that money on a commercial and their survey doesn't even meet the rigorous standards demanded by *Family Fortunes*! How odd.

Once I've noticed something like this it starts to prey on my mind. It gets under my skin. I get a little obsessed. We watched the rest of the episode but I couldn't concentrate on another word the Belgian detective said. I spent the whole time wondering if Rimmel's advertising was always as statistically odd as that. Was the small print always that strange?

I was still thinking about it when I woke up the next morning … so while I waited for my first coffee of the day to brew I thought I'd just take a quick look around the internet and see what I could find. YouTube was the obvious place to start.

It didn't take me long to track down an online version

of the ad from the night before* and others were only a couple of mouseclicks away.

Take, for example, an ad for Rimmel London's Lasting Finish 25 Hour Foundation.**

'*Why 25 hours?*' asks the smooth voiceover man. '*Because you want a foundation to last as long as you do!*'

It's as he says *these* words that the first small print arrives: '*94% of 81 women agreed.*'

I'll be honest. That wasn't as silly a statistic as I'd been hoping for. I know 81 women is a woefully small sample to be using in a hugely expensive ad campaign but it's not as wilfully odd as 99 women. And even if it's based on a small sample, 94 per cent is a pretty impressive stat.

I shrugged, poured the coffee and fetched a box of cereal from the cupboard. And then a thought hit me. Hang on. What had 94 per cent of 81 women agreed to? I went back and watched it again.

The cheeky buggers! The timing with which it appears on the screen suggests that what the 76 women out of 81 are agreeing with is that '*you <u>want</u> a foundation to last as long as you do*'. There's genuinely nothing there to suggest they agree that it *does* last 25 hours. They've basically got a huge approval rating for the notion that it would be desirable for make-up to last as long as the person who's wearing it lasts. Which begs the question: what the hell were the other five women thinking? '*No, I'd like my*

* http://gor.mn/Rimmel1
** http://gor.mn/Rimmel2

make-up to last less time, thank you very much. If it could all disappear an hour or two before I'm finished for the day so that I could look quite blotchy on the night bus, that would be perfect.'

The ad continues.

'Feels hydrating all day!' Says v/o-man. *'Fade proof, transfer proof for up to 25 hours.'*

And it's as he says *these* words that the more meaningful statistic appears: *'73% of 34 women.'*

Hang on. So they put Question 1, *'Do you want your foundation to last as long as you do?'*, to 81 women but Question 2, *'Does it feel hydrating all day and is it fade proof and transfer proof for up to 25 hours?'*, to only 34 women? Did 47 women walk away in disgust at the stupidity? Did the five who didn't want their make-up to last stay with the group or did they leave? Or were they *all* different women and was this a different occasion completely? And while I'm at it, doesn't *'up to 25 hours'* mean *anything-up-to-and-including-25-hours?* If it lasted 25 minutes that would qualify as *'up to 25 hours'*, wouldn't it?

I assume the same 34 women were involved in another survey too.

*'New Rimmel London Volume Booster Lip Gloss! Bring your lips to life. Collagen spheres. Lip plumping sensation. Sexy voluptuous lips,'** says the unseen Mr Rimmel while animated cartoon spheres disappear into Kate Moss's real

---

* http://gor.mn/Rimmel3

lips. The small print confirms that, once again, 34 women have been consulted on this claim.

And guess what percentage of them agreed this time? Drum roll, please. Amazingly, the answer is 47 per cent.

Less than half! More women disagreed than agreed! I mean, they only asked 34 women in the first place so it's not exactly scientific but imagine going back to your boss and having to reveal that only sixteen out of 34 women had agreed and eighteen hadn't.

'It doesn't work!' they must have thought. 'What are we going to do?'

'I know,' an eager young intern will have said. 'We'll just have to go back to the lab and tell the scientists to think again. They can improve the formula, they can make it work.'

'Are you crazy! Do you know how much this research and development stuff costs? Any other ideas?'

'Well … um … maybe we could ask *more* women? Maybe we asked the wrong women. I mean, it's *nearly* half. If we can ask just two more women and they both agree then we'll have eighteen out of 36!'

'Is that half?'

'Yeah!'

'But what if they don't like it?'

'We'll be down to 44 per cent.'

'Are you crazy! We can't risk losing three per cent by asking two more of these stupid bitches. What else can we do?'

'Ummm … I know!'

'What?'

'We could just tell people it makes their lips plumper and let the small print tell them that most people think it doesn't! If we put cartoon collagen spheres on and make it look sciencey they'll believe us. I mean, what's more believable, animated spheres or people?'

Now … brace yourselves. Could it get more ridiculous than 47 per cent of 34?

Yes. Yes. Yes. I'm overjoyed to tell you that it could. Yes!

It's another ad featuring Kate Moss.

'*Rimmel London's new Lasting Finish Minerals Foundation,*' says the voiceover as Kate wanders into a bedroom somewhere in black and white. '*Light as air powder with even cover. 95 per cent skin friendly minerals. Lasts up to twelve hours. Perfect finish.*'*

They're still stubbornly refusing to get involved with a three-figure sample size but this time we're back to a survey of 99 women. But while 71 per cent of 99 women thought that the Match Perfection foundation was undetectable, the number who thought that the Lasting Finish Minerals Foundation would last up to twelve hours is somewhat less impressive.

It's much less impressive. It's so unimpressive it's almost impressive. You have to kind of admire their chutzpah in just going for it.

* http://gor.mn/Rimmel4

It's less than half.

It's less than the previous low of 47 per cent too.

Are you ready for this? Only twenty out of 99 women agreed. Twenty! Out of 99! Basically, four fifths of women disagreed! It's not even close. An overwhelming majority of the people surveyed think this stuff doesn't do what the manufacturer says it does. And apparently it's OK for them to still say it. Because the small print's there to fill you in. Just so long as you're not distracted by Kate Moss. Ooh look ... it's Kate Moss! Isn't she lovely!

CHAPTER 9

• • • • • • • • • • • •

'HEY, BUZZFEED SEEMS TO WORK … LET'S TRY AND BE MORE LIKE BUZZFEED!'

You have probably visited the website, BuzzFeed.com. If you haven't, you have almost certainly visited a site that is trying to copy it. BuzzFeed is a web aggregator. It collects together things that are buzzing around the internet. If something is a viral hit, BuzzFeed has a home for it.

Over time BuzzFeed has acquired a style and a voice of its own. Lists. It loves lists. Here's a selection of genuine BuzzFeed headlines:

> **7 Sexy Things Guys Do Without Realizing It.**

> **8 Things You Learn To Appreciate After Moving Back Home.**

> **10 Problems Only Short Girls Understand.**

> **11 Pairs Of Meggings That Prove That Meggings Should Not Exist.**

> **12 Reasons Why 'Parenthood' Is The Realest Show On TV.**

**16 Strange Things That Have Already Happened
In Local Newspapers This Year.**

18 Celebrities You Didn't Know Were Really Short.

**19 Things People Swear They'll Never Do
Until They Have Kids.**

**Meet The 20 Dogs Who Took Over This Year's
Sundance Film Festival.**

**26 Things You Need To Do Before You
Graduate High School.**

30 Things Guys In Their Thirties Are Afraid To Admit.

38 Bizarre Items Dropped On New Year's Eve.

And that, ladies and gentlemen, is the list I call, 12 BuzzFeed Headlines That Sound Like Parodies But Aren't.

(Oh, and by the way, I had no idea what 'meggings' were either. But I looked them up. They're leggings ... but for men.)

I'm sure some people will regard that assortment of headlines as a dread cluster of vapid, hollow nonsense. But to others it will sound like a collection of unfussy LOLs. I'm not knocking it. If anything I think it's pretty admirable. BuzzFeed are expert manipulators of our culture of Too Much Information. They understand better than most the way the human brain behaves in the never-ending sweet shop of the internet, where new content is only ever a click away. BuzzFeed makes catnip for the short attention span.

A title along the lines of '*25 Cute Pictures Of Cute Things Being Cute*' offers a huge temptation to the bored office worker on a lunch break. The listiness reassures you that it won't take long. It's just there. It's just one click away. And how long can it take to look at 25 pictures on one page? Thirty seconds? And who cares if you don't look at them all anyway? It's not like starting a thousand-word article or anything ... so you click. And you get 25 pictures. And four or five of them weren't that cute actually, but another four or five were really nice and two actually made you chuckle and there's that girl you know who really loves pug dogs so you ought to send her a link because she'll love the seventeenth picture down. So you send her the link and then you look at the page. And you see a dozen other equally tempting links.

'*13 Mice That Look Exactly Like Ant n Dec.*' '*The 19 Sexiest Photos You'll See All Year.*' '*Ten Ways Being Tall Sucks.*' '*38 Photos That Just Don't Make Sense!*' And so on and so on and so on.

It's the disposability of it all that sells it. It's *just* a click. It'll only take a few seconds. It's not going to be very demanding. You'll probably chuckle. OK ... just one more click. Photos. Snarky pop culture. Cute animals. Sexy celebrities. Pith. *That's* what BuzzFeed deals in. They didn't invent it. But they have perfected it. It's a slick machine that lures you in and traps you in its mesh of trivia, raunch, OMGs and LOLs by constantly offering just-one-more-thing. It's the web equivalent of John

Cleese's oleaginous French waiter offering Terry Jones's corpulent and vomitous Mr Creosote 'a *waffer* thin mint' in Monty Python's *The Meaning Of Life*, and one day someone's brain will explode from the excess.

But it works. Boy does it work. A January 2013 *Business Insider* article* valued the company at $200 million, said its revenue for 2012 was likely to be $20 million – triple what it made in 2011 – and suggested investors were hoping it would eventually sell for upwards of $600 million. No wonder so many other sites are copying its house style. Or as a BuzzFeed writer would probably put it: '*The 600 Million Reasons Every Other Site Is Trying To Be Like BuzzFeed!*'

You might remember the solicitous email from someone called Alex trying to lure me into the evil MyLikes network. One of his suggested links was for a '*15 Most "Bro" Colleges*' article. What was that if not a piss-poor attempt to ape BuzzFeed's house style?

And they're not the only ones. BuzzFeed has been so successful that it now seems *everyone* else is trying to copy it. I don't mind BuzzFeed. Good luck to them. But I do resent the BuzzFeedification of everything else.

I am an awful procrastinator. No. That's not right. I am an excellent procrastinator. If you're looking to hire someone to procrastinate for you, I'm your man. I'm really good at it. But I'll have to check my emails first.

---

* http://gor.mn/biBzzFd

One of the things that makes me so good at procrastinating is that I'm as likely to be distracted by things I don't like as I am by the things I do. I was chasing a deadline on some writing three days ago. Because I knew that I had to send a finished piece over to an editor by five o'clock that afternoon I was being strict with myself. I hadn't opened Twitter. I hadn't looked at Facebook. I hadn't even checked my emails. I was trying to be good.

Because I was trying to be good, the one distraction I told myself I was allowed was news.

I have a friend who says he doesn't drink and yet he is regularly sloshed. If you challenge him on it he responds, *'Ah, but it wasn't a fizzy lager or some cheap plonk ... it was a fine wine. Fine wine isn't* drinking*! It's not about getting drunk. I'm a connoisseur!'*

Well, that's my argument with news. Reading news isn't proper procrastination. News is good. News is healthy. News is a socially responsible thing to consume. I am a connoisseur!

So I had a cup of tea, two biscuits and an internet full of news. My plan was to catch up with the headlines – just to take in enough news to make me feel like a functioning, adult citizen of the world – until my cup ran dry and *then* start work. Or rather ... then make a second cup of tea and *then* start work.

So that's what I was doing. I promise you, it wasn't the fizzy-lager, shallow showbiz news. I wasn't reading tittle-tattle. It was proper news. Real news. Grown-up news.

The kind of news you wouldn't mind Facebook telling your friends you're reading.

At the end of one particular story of political intrigue and import, a collection of links had been gathered together in an *if-you-liked-that-you-might-also-like-this* way. These links included, *'The 15 Coolest Facts About Richard Branson'** and *'The 23 Photoshop Fails of the X Factor 2013 Finalists'.***

Now I'm not particularly interested in Richard Branson and I struggle to understand in what way a fact can be cool. And I hadn't been following *X Factor* so I didn't know who the finalists were and probably wouldn't be best placed to appreciate the 'Photoshop fail' photos.

And yet I still clicked on the bloody links. Why? I'll tell you why. Because I wanted to be annoyed by them. Because I thought the whole *if-you-liked-that-you-might-also-like-this* way of presenting these links was disingenuous. I thought they were precisely the kind of things that someone reading proper news was likely to be uninterested in and so, fuelled by some pointless sense of righteous indignation, I clicked on them in order to prove myself right.

Which makes me a silly tit. But there you go.

'The 23 Photoshop Fails of the X Factor 2013 Finalists' was a truly remarkable piece of wannabe-BuzzFeed

---

* http://gor.mn/15Branfacts
** http://gor.mn/XFctrPSfail is the link to visit if you want to see where the article used to be …

writing that left my jaw slack with wonder. (I say 'was' because it seems it no longer exists. Four or five days after Yahoo first published it to their showbiz pages, it disappeared. We'll probably never know *why* it disappeared. It could be that the powers-that-be in the *X Factor* camp gently persuaded them to remove it … but it seems just as likely that the author of the piece died of shame and they took it down as an act of sympathy.)

It's easy to see how the piece was first conceived but impossible to understand how it got beyond the ideas stage and on to our screens. After five minutes' thought somebody should have been saying, '*No … it won't work … let's do something else.*'

Here's the situation:

A new series of *X Factor* had recently begun. The show had run a big photo shoot for all its remaining contestants and sent all of the resulting shots to every outlet that deals with that particular shade of showbiz. The people at Yahoo wanted to run them. But they needed an angle. In an ideal world, they wanted to add some snark. Because snark – as tiresome as it is – is the currency in which all pop culture must be traded these days. Everyone is an ironist. Everyone is aloof. Nobody is a fan. Nobody dares to show their hand and admit to just liking something. Snark rules.

There is a glimmer of hope when someone at Yahoo spots that one of the pictures they've been sent isn't actually a group shot of the aspiring boy band but a series of individual photos that has been rather too hastily stitched together. As a result some of the band appear to have no feet. This is a classic 'Photoshop fail'.

'I know!' the bright Yahoovian spark must have said, 'Let's look at all the photos and see what other Photoshop fails we can find! That way we can run all of the pictures and instead of feeling like we're Simon Cowell's lapdogs, we'll be arch observers of the cultural milieu.'

So 'Photoshop fails' it is. And why not? After all, Photoshop fails are a mainstay of this kind of online meme-tease. On BuzzFeed you'll find articles headlined, '23 Cringeworthy Magazine Cover Photoshop Fails' and '27 Cringeworthy Types Of Photos That Prove No One Should Be Allowed To Use Photoshop'. Not to mention, 'Not-So-Sexy Photoshop Fail', 'Proof Men Shouldn't Be Allowed To Use Photoshop', '17 People Who Need To Get Better At Photoshop', '29 People Caught Photoshopping Their Own Photos' and '37 Professional Photoshoppers Who Should Be Fired Immediately'.

All of those articles are about spotting where photo-editing software has been used badly by people and all of them have been popular. I can see why. When people edit photographs they're telling visual lies and everyone loves seeing a liar caught out. A scrawny kid that thinks using Photoshop will fool the sexy ladies of Facebook into thinking he has a six-pack? That's funny. Someone in the publishing industry – an industry that thrives by creating unrealistic images of beauty for us all to aspire to – being so focussed on their efforts to artificially slim a model's hips that they haven't noticed they've left a disembodied hand floating in space? That's funny too. The appeal of the Photoshop fail is all about seeing the vain and the scheming tripped up by their own incompetence.

But Yahoo have set themselves an impossible task. If you look at the '*23 Cringeworthy Magazine Cover Photoshop Fails*' article on BuzzFeed,* you'll see that every one of the covers they've listed has been culled from a variety of other websites. They'd already been spotted by other people. They'd already been posted online in a variety of places. All BuzzFeed have done is gather them together, post them on one page, counted them and then put that number in the title. They had the whole of the internet to search and they found 23 examples they thought were worth including.

Yahoo have tried to come up with something similar, but with a much smaller pool of photos to work from. They've got the results of one photo shoot to work with. And most of the photos *haven't* been 'shopped. They should have killed the idea when they realised as much … but they didn't let the lack of examples get in their way, they just ploughed on regardless.

As a result they end up tying themselves in knots. There are several occasions where, instead of pointing out where Photoshop has been used badly, the article ends up

* http://gor.mn/23Mag

crowing about where it should have been used but hasn't! They've reinterpreted '*Photoshop fail*' to mean '*failure-to-use-Photoshop*'. 'You can see some muddy footprints on the floor!' they squawk. 'You can see the line where the floor meets the ceiling!' they wail. Instead of catching a liar in the act, they're calling them out for their honesty!

'*Gary Barlow's Groups shot had a number of fails including one very unhappy member of Code 4*', read one of the captions. And they're right. One of the men in the photo does look a little glum. But that isn't a Photoshop fail! That's a photo of a man who just happens not to be smiling.

Instead of being the 'arch observers' they set out to be, they've ended up taking the most industry-centric stance of all. '*These photos should be flawless,*' they gripe. '*If these people want to be famous … these photos should have been Photoshopped properly. Why isn't everyone beautiful? Why are there footprints on the floor? Why isn't everyone smiling? This is a disaster!*'

The article was every bit as awful as I'd thought it would be. It was terrible. I didn't enjoy it at all. But man alive, did I enjoy not enjoying it! I was definitely right. It was appalling. And so my attention turned to '*The 15 Coolest Facts About Richard Branson*'.

Click. Click.

The link led to a site called celebritytoob.com. They obviously take the 'celebrity' part of the brief very seriously as the introduction to this article is all about justifying Branson's place as a legitimate celeb; they wouldn't want anyone to get confused and think they'd ended up reading entrepreneurtoob.com by mistake:

> For those of you who don't know, Richard Branson is the sole owner of the Virgin Group of companies that has plenty of business concerns under its umbrella. He's been in business since before 1970 and he's known as one of the most successful entrepreneurs today. In fact his success is so "public"* that Branson isn't just considered a businessman. He's a well known celebrity to boot. So we decided to do a little digging into the life of Sir Richard to see what we could find that you might be interested in. Here are 15 fun facts about Richard Branson.

You'll notice also that by the end of the introduction the facts are no longer the coolest facts that the link had promised. They are now fun facts. Mind you, the article is *actually* headlined '*15 Interesting Facts About Sir Richard Branson*' so there's obviously been a bit of indecision. They're the coolest! No. They're interesting! Hmm. They're fun!

We'll see, shall we? They do go into detail on some of them, but here, for your delectation, is the list in precis:

---

* No. I don't know why this was in inverted commas either.

1. Branson has overcome dyslexia.
2. He dropped out of high school at the age of sixteen.
3. He's one of the five richest people in the UK.
4. He owns an island.
5. He's been awarded by the United Nations.
6. He has two children by his second wife.
7. He's a world-record-winning hot-air balloonist.
8. He's registered the phrase 'Virgin Interplanetary' for future use.
9. He's a car collector.
10. Virgin has over 200 businesses.
11. He called his first business Virgin because it was his first time.
12. He cried when he sold Virgin Records.
13. He's been knighted.
14. He's a family man.
15. If you want to reserve a trip into space on Virgin Galactic, it'll cost you £200,000.

Which of those facts were fun? In what sense *can* a fact be fun? Did you have fun finding out that Virgin has over 200 businesses? Is it cool that he's been knighted? I'm not sure that Number 2 is *even* a fact. After all, sixteen is the age at which people leave high school. They're only two facts into a fifteen fact list and I'm pretty sure they're already failing the fundamental requirement of factiness.

Number 7 probably deserves greater scrutiny too.

Here's the fuller version:

7. Hot Air Balloon World Record – In 1987 Branson broke the world record for being the first and only person to cross the Atlantic in the largest hot air balloon! Following this, in 1991 he again broke his own record by crossing 6700 miles of the Pacific in a Virgin hot air balloon.

What does this mean? If you hold the world record for being the first person to cross the Atlantic, you don't *beat* that record by *also* crossing the Pacific. What was it a record for? The longest hot-air balloon flight? The longest sea crossing by hot-air balloon? The largest balloon? And whatever it was, he's not the first and only person to do something because he didn't do it alone. He was accompanied by Per Lindstrand on both occasions.

There's more.

9. He's a Car Collector – Owning priceless vintage pieces like the Morris Mini Minor and the Humber Super Snipe, the Virgin leader loves to invest in pricey yet elegant collectables. Still though, he normally drives around in a Range Rover.

I just checked and, as I type, you can get a 1967 Humber Super Snipe – with a full MOT – for £6,000 and a Morris Mini Minor for a little less than that. These are very much *not* priceless. They have a price. And it's about six grand apiece. And if Richard Branson does love to invest in pricey yet elegant collectables why, in a 2010 interview,* did he say the following? *'I don't actually own a car! Living on a Caribbean island there's not really much call for one. Most recently, I did own a Land Rover when I was spending more time in the UK.'*

Oh man. Fact-checking is really taking the fun right out of these fun facts. I'm such a spoilsport.

It gets weirder, mind.

13. He's been Knighted. You probably knew that already given his "Sir" status. But did you know that Branson is a regular joker and makes fun of himself all the time? It's proven by the fact he's been on the show Friends as well as Baywatch. And we're sure you've seen some of his commercials.

What is the fact here? That he's been knighted or that he's a joker? And what is the connection between the two? Why are they sharing a paragraph? Does anyone get the feeling that they're running out of ideas?

But there's an even more wonderful example still to come.

14. He's a family man. Despite his success in business, according to a British poll, he is one of

* http://gor.mn/Bransoniv

those few men, after Mother Teresa, who could
be eligible to write the Ten Commandments.

This is my very favourite fact. Mainly because I have no idea what it's supposed to mean. I'm British. I don't remember that poll. Maybe I was on holiday when we had that *Who Are The Few Men After Mother Teresa Who Could Be Eligible To Write The Ten Commandments?* referendum.

The whole thing reeks of cut-and-paste. Could you really describe this article as having been 'written'? Not in any meaningful sense of the word, surely? It's been stitched out of fragments that someone's found littering the internet, hasn't it?

What you need to remember here is that I was offered this link on a serious news page! What financial arrangement exists to persuade them to prick-tease its readers with this tosh?

What is that doing in an *if-you-liked-that-you-might-also-like-this* tease?

'Hey you … you're reading a news story that's been written and researched by a professional journalist … and that makes me think you might also be interested in this thing put together by someone who has a greater command of Google than they do the English language. Some of it's true and some of it isn't and all of it is very badly written … but it doesn't really matter. Of course, once you click on it, you'll leave our website – the one you came to because you wanted some news – but at

least we'll make a few pennies and maybe you'll come back another time ... see ya!'

Is it really worth it to them? Maybe they don't see it as any different to any other advert? If someone advertises a vacuum cleaner on their site nobody assumes they're endorsing it so why should this be any different? Well, because *they are* endorsing it that's why. They're the ones saying *if-you-liked-that-you-might-also-like-this*. That text sits outwith the adverts. It isn't written in the advertiser's voice, it comes direct from the site and they should bloody well know better.

If you were in a high-end restaurant and the waiter approached you at the end of your meal to say, '*I can see you enjoyed that so I hope you won't mind me recommending somewhere else you might like,*' you'd expect him to recommend a place with similar culinary qualities. If you followed his recommendation a week later and discovered it was a rat-infested, blood-stained kebab van you'd be more than a little confused. So when a site that offers professional writing recommends some other writing to you, I think they should check that it meets their own standards. Because when *they* tell me that they think *I* will like it, I hold *them* to account when I don't.

But this is what it's come to. Surely we're only a stone's throw away from the news sites themselves just joining in. Can it be long before the *Guardian* publishes '*37 Hotels That Look Just Like Josef Stalin*', *The Times* runs with '*The 12 Pictures That Prove Natasha Kaplinsky Knows Something*

You Don't Know' and the *Telegraph* goes with *'10 Cats Respond To The Labour Party Conference'*.

Actually. That stone has been thrown. I only made two of those up. The *Telegraph* has published *'10 Cats Respond To The Labour Party Conference'*.* Ten stock pictures of cats. Ten snarky comments about the Labour Party conference. It exists. The end is nigh.

* http://gor.mn/10CatsTlgrph

CHAPTER 10

• • • • • • • • • • •

IF SPAMMERS WERE BETTER AT SPAMMING THEY WOULDN'T SEND ANYWHERE NEAR AS MUCH SPAM

People collect all sorts of odd things. I know people who collect thimbles, matchbooks, football cards and even second-hand photographs of women and dogs. (But not like *that*.) Me? I have a large collection of spam emails. As collections go, it has some benefits. They're free, they take up hardly any space and they couldn't be easier to find. In fact, really, they just come to you.

I'm being facetious. But only just. You see, many years ago, I made a mistake. In a spirit of openness, I decided it would be a good idea to put my email address on my website. That wasn't a good idea. It was a very bad idea. Spammers have all sorts of ways of getting hold of your email address – posting it online where anyone can see it was just making their job easier.

Clever software automatically scours the internet, searching for email addresses. When it finds the @ symbol it simply scrapes the text either side of it and adds it to the list. Job done.

By treating that email address with abandon I was tacitly encouraging others to do the same and it wasn't long before it could be found on a dozen or more other websites. You can't put the genie back in the bottle. It's out there. It's been shared. Added to lists. Bought and sold by spammers all over the world. In fifteen years, I reckon it has probably received around 20,000 legitimate emails ... but in the same time, I have calculated that it has received more than twenty million spam emails. If that sounds far-fetched, bear in mind that at its peak it was being sent between 30,000 and 40,000 such emails in a day. At that rate, it would top ten million in just a year.

It didn't matter what filters were put in place, enough spam would always bleed through to make it all but impossible to find and deal with the legitimately sent correspondence and so, with regret, I eventually gave up on it. I created a new email address (one that I handle with a bit more discretion) and gave the old one up for good.

Or at least that was the idea. In truth, I have never quite been able to let go. I still have the password. And from time to time I still log on and look at the inbox. I don't do it out of any noble sense that I might just catch something that has been sent in good faith, I do it because I find it all so grimly fascinating.

So you see, I really do collect spam emails. Kind of.

In a way. In that I maintain an inbox that now exists for no reason other than to be a chamber of spam-horrors. Lifting the lid and peering in is always just a little thrilling. As if I'm flirting with danger. Deep in my gut I harbour an irrational fear that it will turn out like that scene at the end of *Raiders of the Lost Ark*, when the Nazis open the Ark of the Covenant and unleash the angels of death. Of course it never turns out like that and instead I just find myself gawping in wonder at all that has gathered there.

In a certain mood, some spam can appear strangely admirable. In a movie, a conman can be a hero or a villain as the plot demands. Put him in a sharp suit and make the people he cons venal, avaricious types with more money than sense and the audience will root for him. Better still, make him a her. Dress her in a figure-hugging cocktail dress and make the marks fat, old, rich perverts and the audience will love watching her wrap them round her little finger. You can view spam through the same lens if you choose. How ingenious some of it appears!

Of course, in reality the charming, heroic and sexy conmen and women of the silver screen don't really exist. Con-people don't pick and choose morally appropriate targets. Of course they don't; they prey on the vulnerable. And the same is surely true of the spammers who cast their nets wide in the hope that someone, somewhere will fall for it. They're all villains, really.

The spam that fascinates me the most is the spam that

blends clever and stupid. This is the spam that leaves your jaw slack with twofold wonder, first at the notion that the person who sent it thought someone was going to fall for it ... and then at the certain knowledge that somewhere on earth exists a person stupid enough to do so.

Penis enlargement is a classic spam topic. That it works as a tactic at all speaks volumes about the insecurity of men. A lot of them arrive at my spam farm. I don't take it personally. But they make a useful example for illustrating the ludicrous nature of spam. In one two-minute window, I was sent two dozen such emails from a company offering me a product called *Megadik*.

The text in the emails followed a pattern. The core message – delivered in just two sentences – was the same, but in each email, certain words had been substituted with synonyms. Well, synonyms after a fashion at any rate. For example, the most coherent version opened with the following:

Girls always laughed at me, and even men did in the public toilets.

While another would start:

Cuties always hee hawed at me, and even gents did in the municipal wc.

You get the picture. And the second sentence was given the same treatment. So there was the straightforward:

> Well now I laugh at them because I took MegaDik
> for 6 months and now my penis is much longer
> than most.

And also the downright eccentric:

> Well now I ha-ha at them because I took Me_ga_D.ik
> for 14 months and now my flute is badly more than
> civil.

I know that they're changing the wording in the hope that they'll evade spam-detection software, but what's the point of that if the message that eventually gets through is basically gobbledegook?

Reading the emails in sequence is like watching the world's hardest game of *Blankety Blank* go horribly awry.

> Blank always blanked at me, and even blank did in
> the blankety blank. Well now I blank at them because
> I took blank for blank months and now my blank is
> blanker than blank.

Hmm, I've gone with:

> Dames always whooped at me, and even chaps did in

the open john. Well now I whoop at them because I took m.e.g.a.dik for 9 months and now my pride is quite preponderant than Joe.

I collated the various options used in the emails I received. As well as girls, cuties and dames, they used blondes, ladies, dolls, females, cats, maidens and – my particular favourite – baronesses. The idea that a man might have a penis that is *always* reducing baronesses to laughter is just wonderful!

Not that they do always *laugh*. As you know, sometimes they hee haw and sometimes they whoop. Well, on other occasions they also titter, snigger, giggle, shriek, smile, tee hee, ha ha and – wait for it – whizgiggle. Yes. Whizgiggle! Damn those baronesses and their incessant whizgiggling!

The men, gents and chaps were also gentlemen, lords, youths, fellows, rascals and – I wish I was making this up – highwaymen. I'm guessing the people sending these emails didn't speak English as a first language, but even so, it's hard to imagine quite how they looked for a synonym for 'men', stumbled upon 'highwaymen' and thought, 'Yeah … that'll do.'

As you know, the location for the women's mirth is sometimes called a public toilet, a municipal WC or an open john. But it went by other names. Like unrestricted toilet, free comfort station, national bathroom, not-private WC, open wee house and the bizarrely Anglo-French construction, loo publique.

And so it goes on.

Well, now I laugh/hee haw/whoop/snigger/giggle/shriek/smile/tee hee/ha ha/whizgiggle at them because I took Megadik/m.e.g.a.dik/Me.ga.dik/Me_ga_d.ik for 3/4/5/6/7/9/14 months and now my penis/cock/shaft/putz/tool/flute/flesh/pride/trumpet/schlong/trouser-mouse is much longer/badly more/quite preponderant/excessively longer/excessively greater/very much greater/much best/indeed greater/excessively weightier/badly more/pro-massive than most/civil/Joe/world/national/average/public-level.

In what way do these different versions actually help them to get a response?

Try if you can to imagine someone receiving – and falling for – the most straightforward form of the email.

Girls always laughed at me, and even men did in the public toilets. Well now I laugh at them because I took MegaDik for 6 months and now my penis is much longer than most.

Imagining this person involves imagining someone who believes that a pharmaceutical company has developed a pill or cream that has been proven to permanently increase the size of a singular part of a man's anatomy. For some reason this development hasn't made the news and the pharmaceutical company responsible have eschewed the idea of selling it in high-street chemists. No, they'd rather keep it all a bit hush-hush. Instead they're marketing it by emailing random individuals.

Now I think it's pretty hard to imagine such a person existing. But we have to assume they exist.

Now take your imaginary person – this person whose existence has stretched your imagination to breaking point with their barely believable doltish credulity – but set them a different test. This time, imagine them reading one of the alternative emails. This one says:

> Baronesses always whizgiggled at me, and even highwaymen did in the open wee house. Well now I whizgiggle at them because I took M.e.g.a.Dik for 5 months and now my trouser mouse is pro-massive than national.

Is your imaginary dunderhead still falling for it? What if he's received two dozen of these emails in an instant? Are they backing each other up or are they undermining one another? What if they were all sent by different email addresses – each one with an almost identical name? Catalina B. Spicer, Catalina M. Spicer, Catalina Q. Spicer and so on.

Nobody could possibly take them at face value, could they? Here are the options:

Option 1:

The person who sent these emails is clearly dishonest and therefore untrustworthy and almost certainly not the kind of person I should give my credit card details to.

Option 2:

Mr and Mrs Spicer are an eccentric pair. They had a lot of daughters and named them all Catalina! Perhaps this has given the girls an unusually close bond. That would explain why they've all sought work at the same employer: the strangely private, almost secret, penis-enlargement firm. I imagine having a lot of employees with almost identical names must make it confusing at work. Maybe that explains why they've all emailed me this morning. Someone must have left a note reminding 'Catalina Spicer' to email me and they've all bloomin' well done it! It is odd that some of them have a decent grasp of English and yet others don't. I wonder why 'R' thinks it's a bad thing that cats always smile at someone? That sounds nice to me ...

Chapter 11

• • • • • • • • • • • •

ALGORITHM & BLUES

On 23 August 2013 I became aware that Chas Hodges – the piano-playing half of rockney duo Chas 'n' Dave – was on Twitter. Being a fan of his music, I followed him.

Twitter responded by sending me the following message:

You might also want to follow @NoelGallagher & @KylieMinogue

This is not a conversation a human being would ever have. Nobody in the history of the world has ever looked through a friend's record collection and said, 'I see you like your Chas 'n' Dave. I bet you're really into Oasis and Kylie too, aren't you?'

Never.

Chapter 12

. . . .

BUYING A RECORD IS NOT A FORM
OF PROTEST

If Chapter 5 proved one thing it is this: your author is an old man.

I'm sure young people will have read that thinking, '*Durr … what about downloads? Why don't people just download the specific tracks they want? Who's paying for an actual CD these days?*'

They have a point. I am of the generation that likes *stuff*. Actual stuff. Physical objects. I like owning books. I like owning CDs and DVDs. I know that I only need my eyes, ears and brain to consume them but I like to hold them. Hell, with books, I sometimes find I like to smell them too.* I can't help it. I like to hold the object. I like to feel its heft in my hand.

I do have a Kindle. I like my Kindle. It is incredibly handy when I'm travelling. But it's not the same as holding a book. I am increasingly likely to download

---

* Someone should definitely find a way of making a Kindle smell of books.

music too. But I still enjoy leafing through the sleeve notes of a CD.

I'm sure future generations will view this need for the physical form as odd. '*But where did you keep it all?*' they will ask. '*I mean,* how big *were your houses?*'

I can see the tide has turned. I should probably just give in to it and commit to living an even more digital life. And maybe one day I will. But I'm not there yet. Not yet.

When it comes to music, I'm jealous of children today. I know I'm meant to say the opposite – that we had proper bands when I was young and they have Justin Bieber, Wand Erection,* and whoever's won the most recent series of *X Factor* – but I think that's too simplistic a view.

When I was a kid the nearest we had to downloading free music was taping songs off the radio. The quality was dreadful. If you wanted to cut out the babbling DJ you had to be able to press the play and record buttons with ninja-like precision and even when you got it half right, all you really had was a piece of tape that would slowly stretch and distort, rendering it unlistenable within a year or two.

But records were expensive. Buying a single felt almost impossibly exciting. But an album? An album was out of this world! It involved a real commitment – two or three weeks' pocket money had to be saved to buy an album – and so every duff track would be bitterly resented. In

---

* I know, I know …

fact it was worse than that; every duff track would be *denied*. The emotional and financial commitment involved in buying an LP was so great you would convince yourself that you loved every single second of it *no matter what*. I couldn't tell my parents that I'd found the two or three inevitable filler tracks a bit dull! That would be like telling them I'd stood in the street and set fire to my pocket money. The very thought was too much to bear so instead I would pretend to myself – as well as to them – that the eight-minute drum solos and discordant sound-poems were exactly what I was after. I had to. Because it was *an album*.

Was that situation really better than that faced by teen-agers today? Music is cheaper. Music is often – legally *and* illegally – free. It is a much more disposable commodity and while that might mean that individual tracks aren't treated with reverence, it also means that more music is consumed. And old duffers like me shouldn't be distracted by the Beliebers' screams or the Erectioners'* wails. Every generation has someone to scream at and pledge their devotion to. It's a soap opera that carries them along on its eddies and tides and of course a few of them get swallowed up whole by it. Some of them will feel a depth of love for Justin B that will be all-consuming for a while. And then one day, they'll emerge into the real world, blinking like pit ponies, unsure how to process who they

---

* I know.

were and what they were thinking. But they're the minority. The very vocal, screaming minority. For many more, that's just the surface and it's unlikely to be the sum total of what they listen to. The vast array of music online means so much more can be explored and the teenagers I meet tend to listen to a far broader range of stuff than I ever did at that age. Of course they listen to the bands that are on the magazine covers and Radio 1 playlist, but they also listen to Abba, The Beatles, David Bowie, T-Rex, Captain Beefheart, Bob Dylan, Cat Stevens and Frank Zappa. And much, much more. But there's no fun to be had in screaming at old guys. Or dead guys.

TV shows like *The X Factor* are a part of the soap opera. Each series creates a new screamee, a star that will burn brightly – and most often, briefly. And it doesn't matter to the show's producers if their new star's career only lasts six months because the process is always just about to be repeated. There'll be another one along in a minute. It's a win–win situation for them.

'Second screen viewing' is the television industry's phrase of the moment. Or at least it was for a moment while I was writing this book. The second screen is that of your iPad, laptop or smartphone. If a TV show gets a lot of people tweeting, it has a lot of second screen viewers.

The X Factor is one such show. It's not exactly appointment-to-view[*] TV in our house – as I've already

[*] A former TV industry phrase of the moment for you.

said, I wasn't following the most recent series – but I have watched it in the past and I doubtless will again. For me, the pleasure in that kind of show is in the knowledge that others are sharing the experience. Twitter puts everyone on the same sofa for an hour of a Saturday night and there's fun to be had with that.

But what always strikes me as odd is the way in which some of the people who sit there tweeting archly about the delusional contestants and the judges' faux banter end up getting sucked in to the show's orbit.

At the start of a series they're tweeting to ask whether Louis Walsh has dyed his hair or bleached his teeth or both ... but by the end of the series they're tweeting about how appalling it is that Singer X has been kicked off the show while Singer Y remains. *'This is such an injustice,'* they tweet. *'How can Gary Barlow look at himself after saying that!'* *'Fix!'* *'Not fair!'*

At this stage I find myself looking on in dismay. How did all these people – smart grown-ups, it appears – end up caring about who wins this thing?

I understand that millions of people care. I understand that hundreds of thousands of people will actually spend money voting on the outcome. I just assumed that the people tweeting dry comments about how manufactured it all is were the least likely to do so. At what point in the series does their subtext become their text?

Here's my handy guide to working out whether you should or shouldn't care about who wins *The X Factor*:

Have you bought, *for your own enjoyment*, a single by the winner of the *most recent series* of *The X Factor*?

Yes ☐ **No** ☐

Are you ever likely to?

Yes ☐ **No** ☐

If you've ticked one or more yeses, then by all means get yourself worked up into a lather about any perceived injustice on the show. Have a favourite. Cheer when they get through. Be sad when they don't. That's exactly what the show is about. It's for you. Without any prejudice on my part, I encourage you to enjoy the experience as fully as you can.

If however you've ticked two nos, then you need to get a grip. The show *isn't* for you. Caring about who wins a competition to sing a song you won't buy is like caring about whether or not the diner at the table next to you in a restaurant has chosen the right wine to accompany his main course. It's not your problem. Relax.

Of course, there are other ways of getting sucked into the show's orbit. I am just as confused by those who have gone the other way and decided that the show is an entity that must be opposed in some way.

For many years, the *X Factor* winner was almost guaranteed to secure the coveted Christmas number one

spot.* The winners of series two, three, four and five –
Shayne Ward, Leona Lewis, Leon Jackson and Alexandra
Burke – all achieved it, but as the end of series six
approached, there was a groundswell of opinion that said:
we can make this stop.

And they did. A Facebook and Twitter campaign saw
huge numbers of people download 'Killing In The Name'
by Rage Against The Machine to beat *X Factor* winner
Joe McElderry's single, 'The Climb', into second place.

There was much celebration and talk of people power.
But I'm afraid the whole thing left me feeling a little
baffled.

I can think of only one reason for buying a piece of
music. I buy a piece of music because I like it and would
like to own it. I buy a piece of music in order to add it to
my collection.

I am writing these words on a warm September afternoon. I can cheerfully say that at no point this year have
I been even remotely aware of who or what is at number
one in the charts. I don't care what is in the charts right
now, I didn't care yesterday, I won't care tomorrow and
I'll be damned if I can muster the energy to start caring
come Christmas. Of course buying a single has an influence on its chart position but influencing its chart position
isn't a sensible motivation for buying a single. It makes as

* An ancient law forbids writing about the notion of a Christmas
number one without referring to it as the 'coveted Christmas number
one spot'.

much sense to me as choosing your fabric softener because you want to affect the share price of Procter & Gamble.

Of course this is just my opinion and you're perfectly welcome to care about these things if you see fit. If you tune in to a top 40 countdown every week then that's OK, the charts are a part of your personal soap opera. Most of us have one. For me it's the football results. Or the darts. For others it might be local politics, a Neighbourhood Watch scheme or *The Great British Bake Off*. The people I struggle to understand are the ones who spend 51 weeks of the year not giving a fig about what is or isn't a number one and then suddenly decide they want to spend their own money influencing it at Yuletide. Do the chocolates stashed inside their advent calendars contain hallucinogens? What tradition is it they're defending exactly? The Christmas number one in 1971 was 'Ernie, The Fastest Milkman In The West' by Benny Hill. In 1980 it was the St Winifred's School Choir with 'There's No One Quite Like Grandma'. And let's not forget the song 'Mr Blobby' scooping the top spot for Christmas 1993. Although I can't remember who that one was by.

During that Rage Against *The X Factor* campaign, I met and spoke with several people – people in their 40s, no less – who bought three or four copies of 'Killing In The Name' because they 'wanted to do their bit'. At least one of them owned a copy of the song long before the campaign began but still went out and bought it again. And again. And again.

But because so much was written about the campaign, there was also an army of children badgering their parents for extra pocket money so they could fight back by buying Joe McElderry's single more than once too.

What part of that equation do the protestors think Simon Cowell was pissed off by exactly? The record company is in the business of selling records. The more they sell the more money they make. Would they rather sell 400,000 copies and score a number one or 450,000 and get a number two? I'm pretty sure I know the answer.*

The campaign left me feeling like a bunch of rowdy grown-ups had gatecrashed a kid's birthday party in order to point out that the clown was shit. Well done everyone. Did it not occur to you that the clown wasn't actually *for* you?

Did everyone who took part really believe they were defending the sanctity of the Christmas number one? That's what people told me. That's what they told themselves. I suspect it was really about something far more personal than that. In a world full of noise, it must have been fun to be heard. It must have been fun to be part of a movement. For a couple of weeks their drums sounded louder than the rest. For a couple of weeks they were the noise.

* It's not even as though Joe McElderry's single failed to get to number one. It did top the charts. It just didn't get there until the week after Christmas. It was a platinum-selling single – the fifth highest-selling single of the year in the UK.

Did it actually chip away at the *X Factor* edifice? I don't think so. If anything I think it served to aggrandise and embolden it. Is *The X Factor* important to me? No. Do I care what single reaches number one? No. Does it matter to me that the winner of *The X Factor* gets a number one? Of course not. If it *does* matter to you that the winner of *The X Factor* might get to number one then surely it follows that you *do* care about the charts *and* you *do* think *The X Factor* is important.

One day, when the *X Factor* franchise has finally been consigned to history, people will look back on it and use as evidence for its cultural impact the fact that in 2009 hundreds of thousands of people tried to oppose it. I'd rather not have thrown them that scrap, personally.

Mind you, if Simon Cowell gets round to publishing another autobiography, please do start a campaign to get one of my books to Christmas number one ahead of it. I'll be with you all the way.*

---

* In an early draft of this chapter I had initially written, 'Mind you, if Simon Cowell ever publishes an autobiography ...' I changed it when I received an uncharacteristically huffy note from my editor, Jake, telling me about Cowell's 2004 opus, *I Don't Mean to be Rude, But...* 'I can't believe you didn't know about this,' said the note. 'It was a really big book at the time. I'm disappointed, Dave. Shoddy!'

The note was surprising. Jake is normally a much more gentle soul. Two days later I looked the Cowell book up. It turns out that, like me, Simon is published by Ebury. And like me, his editor was ... Jake. Oh, what a tangled web we weave!

CHAPTER 13

• • • • • • • • • • • •

WHY DO THE TWEETS YOU SEE IN SMARTPHONE ADVERTS LOOK NOTHING LIKE THE TWEETS YOU SEE IN REAL LIFE?

Smartphones now rule the world. In early 2013, global sales of smartphones overtook those of their simpler cousins – the feature phones – for the first time prompting the accountancy firm Deloitte to predict that it was the year in which the smartphone would no longer be perceived as a luxury item and would instead be seen as an 'everyday object'.*

This shift in the landscape seems to have started sometime in 2009. Certainly that's when I became aware of a change in the way smartphones were advertised.

Prior to that, a typical print ad for a smartphone would feature a chisel-jawed businessman in a well-tailored business suit doing something business-like-but-dynamic. He

---

* http://gor.mn/Evrydy Quite why an accountancy firm is making predictions about smartphone popularity I don't know. Maybe they'd filed all their clients' tax returns early for once and so had a few days to muck about in the office?

might be hailing a cab outside a train station or boarding an executive jet, that sort of thing. We'd see a close-up of their phone, which would reveal two or three emails with subject lines that teasingly hinted at the kind of life he lived: '*Paris meeting rescheduled for 8am*', '*Sales figures report. Highly confidential*' or '*You are a very powerful and important man*'. OK, maybe not that last one, but you get the gist. It was pretty clear what their target market was.

But in 2009 the advertising changed. Suddenly the suits were gone. And the big sales push was all about how well the phone could integrate with social media. They no longer showed a person holding the phone at all, preferring to go for nothing but a close-up of the phone itself, where, instead of important business emails for important business people, we saw whimsical Facebook status updates and wry tweets. We didn't need to see whose phone this was. We could work out what they were like from the look of their Facebook friends and the people they followed on Twitter. And obviously we were meant to think they were cool. Because we were meant to want to be like them.

The 'friends' in these ads were all attractive. But not threateningly so. They were successful. But not intimidatingly so. They were young, they were cool, they were vibrant and they were living the life. The message, across all of the brands and all of the ads was the same: if you owned *this* phone, you too could have friends like this!

I don't want to have friends like that. Yes, they are young, cool and vibrant, and yes they are living the life.

But the life they are living is an anodyne one. It is a Stepford Life. It is a life invented by an advertising executive, designed to appeal to as broad a cross-section of people as possible … and therefore it is a life designed to offend no one. And that means the one thing they never do is express an opinion. Which seems weird to me because in my experience the world of social media is overflowing with opinions. Too many opinions. Right and wrong, thoughtful and thoughtless, considered and knee-jerk: opinions drip from every corner of the social networks I inhabit. Sometimes exhaustingly so. But not in smartphone adverts.

In smartphone adverts they are perky and upbeat and, well, just ever so slightly hateful. On posters advertising Blackberry, HTC and Motorola we see people tweeting, *'Getting sushi for lunch… cannot wait!'*, *'Miami here I come!'* and *'Coffee in hand, rushing to the bea…'*

In that last one, the complete tweet doesn't fit on the Motorola's screen, meaning we're left to guess to where exactly the recently caffeinated, pretty girl in a beanie hat is rushing. I *think* we're supposed to imagine it's the beach, but I prefer to think it's the *bear baiting competition*. She looks the sort.

On a Samsung poster we meet the oddly named Rick Stivens who tweets, *'Been so busy with my work and the band. Finally got everyhing back in order.'* You see, Rick's a regular guy – he works a regular nine to five job – but Rick's cooler than your average guy because he's in a band. Oh, and he can't spell. The missing 't' in 'everyhing' isn't my typo, it's the ad's.

If any brand was going to do something different I guess my expectation was that it would be Apple. They're a brand apart. They inspire something beyond simple brand loyalty; something more akin to fandom. They've managed to create their own brand-specific argot and their customers – and the media at large – use it without any hint of self-consciousness. Their rivals make and sell computers, laptops, tablets and phones. Not Apple. No, they make iMacs, MacBooks, iPads and iPhones. We all use those terms quite casually and every time we do we subtly reinforce the idea that Apple products are in a category all of their own. I'm not sure how they've persuaded us to do it, but as a marketing tool it's quite, quite brilliant.

So surely they – the most fashionable tech brand of the moment – wouldn't fall into the same peppy, anodyne Twitter hole? You might think not ... but you'd be wrong. On one Apple poster – an iPad advert – we see three tweets:

@julie_stumbaugh
Just ate the best sandwich. Ever.

@johnson_kate
Can't wait to see my sister tomorrow!

@dolan_kevin
Ran 10km this morning.

Well, aren't they all just great! Isn't their world just lovely and bouncy and happy and nice and aaagggghhh.

I know that in and of themselves these tweets are individually fine. Sort of hollow … but fine. But collectively they seem to describe a weird, 'Pleasant Valley Sunday' world full of iced-latte-drinking, chino-wearing, colour-supplement-reading, architect-designed-loft-apartment-dwelling blandness.

There is, however, one novel aspect to this particular poster. It's the only one I saw during this time to show us anything of the device's notional owner. We don't see their face … but we do see their hands. The poster looks at the iPad as if from the owner's point of view, so we see one hand holding the device and the other hovering over the keypad, mid-tweet. Their tweet reads: *'The sun's out but it's raining! How is that even possible?'*

Just take the details in for a moment. One: The sun is out. Two: But it's raining! Three: How is that even possible? Is this a sentence that someone in the Apple marketing machine thinks is witty? Is this supposed to be pithy? How have they arrived in a position where a tweet that reveals nothing but idiocy is held up as an example? *This*, according to Apple, is the kind of sentence that people who aspire to own iPads aspire to tweet! *This* is a person we're meant to aspire to be! *This* is the person who represents *us* in this advert! They're holding the iPad and we are viewing it from their point of view and it's supposed to make us think, *'I wish that was me. That life would be my life if I owned an iPad.'*

Really? I don't find it all that persuasive. It's bad enough that they appear to be following nothing but over-enthusiastic, hyperbolic sandwich-eaters, over-sharing sister-lovers and smug long-distance runners, but on top of that they appear to have no idea how weather works. Didn't they learn this stuff at junior school? I did.

'*The sun's out but it's raining!*' Yes. This is normal. '*How is that even possible?*' Well, um, y'know … rain falls from clouds and sometimes clouds obscure the sun, but not always so, um, y'know, sometimes the rain is falling at the same time as the sun is shining. Does that help?

Perhaps the real message of the ad is: '*Look, iPads can't be that expensive because even this idiot can afford one.*' This plague of stupidity was everywhere in 2009. It wasn't unusual to see four or five consecutive posters on a train station platform all advertising different brands of mobile phone and all using equally vapid examples of social media to do so. I started to become vaguely obsessed with them as a genre. I started photographing them as I encountered them so that I could catalogue their inanities. And as I did so I started to wonder who these people were. At first I'd assumed they were just created in Photoshop for the sake of the adverts. But then a worrying thought landed and it started to gnaw away at my brain. What if they weren't fake? What if they were real?

When a smartphone ad showed music being played it would always namecheck a real song by a real artist. And when they showed a book being read, they always showed real titles by real authors. So why wouldn't the social networkers be real too? Maybe the advertising executives hadn't invented them. Maybe they'd just searched Twitter looking for real people with that special vanilla-vibe and co-opted their tweets? I had to find out so I searched for them on Twitter – and to my amazement, the accounts were all there. Real accounts existed in those names. It's just … well … they weren't all that convincingly real.

If we take a look at two of the accounts that appeared on the iPad poster I mentioned earlier – @julie_stumbaugh and @johnson_kate – and see what they tweeted in just a couple of months you'll see what I mean.

On 3 September Julie Stumbaugh tweeted, '*Just ate the best sandwich. Ever.*' This was followed by 57 days of Twitter silence before she pops up again on 30 October to tweet the exact same words: '*Just ate the best sandwich. Ever.*'

I suppose it's *possible* that Julie spends her life tasting sandwiches and only ever tweets when she's convinced she's finally found the best. Ever. But it seems more likely that the account is simply utilised whenever the marketing people at Apple want to take a photo of one of their products for an ad.

The Kate Johnson account looks much the same but is a little more versatile in that it is used to tweet two phrases. Actually, make that three. They are '*Can't wait to see my sister tomorrow!*' (8 and 17 September and 29 October), '*Ran a 10k this morning*' (2 September) and '*Ran 10 miles this morning*' (8 September).

Ten miles is more than sixteen kilometres so if those tweets aren't for different ads in different markets she must be one hell of a dedicated runner who's able to step up her training regime by 60 per cent in six days. Still, it's nice that her sister pops round so often.

As it happens, a small amount of internet research – and by research I mean putting their names into Google and seeing if anything from LinkedIn shows up – reveals that while the faces you see on these accounts are the faces of models, the names used – Julie Stumbaugh, Kate Johnson, Kevin Dolan, Janielle Penner, Alex Newson and Gage Bock are all names you might see in Apple's blandvertising – are the real names of people who were working for Apple's ad agency, TBWA\Media Arts Lab, at the time the ads were shot.

It isn't just Apple that do this. The account that tweets *'Getting sushi for lunch... cannot wait!'* in the Blackberry ad is in the name of Greg Stark. There's a real Twitter account in that name. It has a model's photo attached to it and appears to largely tweet things that will make good copy for Blackberry adverts. And on LinkedIn there's a real Greg Stark who's a Senior Carrier Ranging Proposition Manager – whatever that is – at Blackberry.

What about Samsung? The company whose advert had given us Rick Stivens? The man who had finally got *everyhing* back in order?

I searched for his name on Twitter. Twitter came back saying, 'No people results for Rick Stivens.' I searched

LinkedIn for Rick Stivens. 'Sorry, no results containing all your search terms were found.'

He didn't seem to exist in either the real or the virtual world. That seemed odd. I checked my photo of the ad to see that I was spelling the name correctly. I was. R, I, C, K, space, S, T, I, V, E, N and S. It was definitely not there. Hmmm. Suddenly I could see why Apple, Blackberry and others had created these shell accounts. It was a good defence mechanism. Because Apple had occupied the account name @Julie_Stumbaugh, nobody else was able to come along use it to mock Apple's products. That would be the last thing they needed.

But Samsung had left that particular door open. There was no @RickStivens account and so there was nothing to stop anyone from creating one. Anyone – and I mean anyone – could do so. It wouldn't take them more than five minutes.

These opportunities don't stay open for long. Sure enough, somebody came along and created a Twitter account in the name of @RickStivens. Not only did they create the account, but because they'd taken photos of smartphone adverts, they were able to give him the same face as that used in Samsung's advertising.

I know. Because I was that somebody. I just couldn't resist. It was just a bit of mischief. And I try to be a nice guy. Which is why, rather than tweeting anything too scurrilous, my first instinct was to just recreate the spirit of Rick Stivens, but to improve his spelling. Which is why the very first tweet I sent out in the name of @RickStivens said, *'Been so busy with my work and the band. Finally got everything back in order.'**

This was a new and improved @RickStivens, an @RickStivens who could spell 'everything' correctly. Not just that, he could spell everything correctly. If you see what I mean.

I sat back and waited for the inevitable email to come.

Dear 'Rick Stivens',

I work for the marketing arm of Samsung and I just wanted to thank you for so realistically recreating the character of Rick Stivens on Twitter for us. We should have thought to create an account on Twitter in his name ourselves … but having made this mistake, it gave everyone a laugh in the office when we saw you had done so instead. We especially appreciate that you haven't used it to tweet anything unpleasant about the brand!

If there's anything we can do for you, just let us know. We'll be happy to help.

Cheers,

Sam Sung

Surely that was the sort of email I'd be receiving, wasn't it? I waited. I'm still waiting.

---

* http://gor.mn/RSTweet1

CHAPTER 14

. . . .

EVERYONE KNOWS WHAT AN APPLE
LOOKS LIKE. DON'T THEY?

For many years, the URL www.dailymail.com led to the website of the Charleston Daily Mail – a daily paper in Charleston, West Virginia. (Not to be confused with the larger and more famous Charleston, South Carolina, the city for which the dance was named.)

I suspect they had an awful lot of hits from people who had turned up looking for the website of the UK's *Daily Mail* – dailymail.co.uk – which for some time now has been the most read newspaper website in the world. I imagine there were hordes of people feeling momentarily put out when they found their computers were showing them information about West Virginian school closures and not pictures of bikini-clad actresses 'showing off their beach bodies' just because they'd gone for a dot-com instead of a dot-co-dot-uk.

By the time you're reading this, I suspect it will all have changed. In December 2013, Associated Newspapers – the company that owns the UK *Daily Mail* – registered as the new owners of the dot-com domain. As I write, it hosts a letter from the American paper explaining that their website has moved to charlestondailymail.com. I imagine it's only a matter of time before the UK lot move in with their confusing brand of titillation-meets-moral-opprobrium. Phwoar, look at the legs on that! How disgusting!

I think most people expect a newspaper's website to be an online version of the print edition. We assume it's much the same thing, but rendered in pixels instead of ink. With some papers that's pretty much true but with the *Mail* I'm not so sure.

MailOnline is a very different beast to the newsprint *Daily Mail*. The content from the paper is on the website, of course, but then so is much, much more. And it's all presented differently. Stories about the stars of obscure American reality shows abound, despite the fact that next-to-nobody in Britain will ever have heard of them.

No British newspaper would bother printing a story about the 'stars' of *Teen Mom* – a reality show about girls who are sixteen and pregnant – for the same reason the *New York Daily Post* doesn't print stories about the cast of *The Only Way is Essex*: because their readers don't watch the shows.

MailOnline has clearly aimed itself at a global audience – and it has succeeded in capturing one.

In truth, I don't think it has a moral agenda. I think it's completely amoral. It's a profit-driven enterprise. It generates hits, it sells advertising. It produces whatever generates the most hits and I very much doubt they care whether you're reading it in a mood of *how-dare-they* outrage or *good-on-them* agreement.

One of the ways the website differs from the paper is in its use of pictures. In the paper, a typical page might contain one or two main stories, and three or four smaller, snappier pieces. Only one of those stories is likely to be accompanied by a photograph. But online, every story has a page of its own. And every story has a photo.

For example, when the paper ran a story about some research done by Portsmouth University into chimpanzees' ability to learn culinary skills by observing other chimps, it was given a small print, five-word headline, 130 words of text and no picture. It had to be treated like that because it was squeezed into the top right-hand corner of page 24. But online that same story was afforded a twenty-word headline, a bullet-pointed summary, 320 words of text, one photo of a chimpanzee and another of celebrity chef Jamie Oliver.

I'd like you to imagine that you work for MailOnline and that your job is finding pictures to accompany the various stories they publish. Sometimes your job is easy. As you'll see in Chapter 30, sometimes a story might as well be, 'We took a photograph of a famous person doing a thing.' When that's the case, the picture selection takes care of itself. But sometimes it's not so simple.

Imagine for example that there's a story about a runaway sheep who's got on to a dual carriageway in North Wales bringing traffic to a standstill. What's really turned it into a story is that a policeman attending the incident handled it not by trying to shepherd the animal to the side of the road but by shooting the sheep with his Taser gun.

You can see why the story is being published: using an electro-shock weapon on an innocent, non-violent sheep seems a little extreme. As one of the motorists who witnessed the incident said, 'I thought it was excessive to use a Taser on a defenceless sheep.'

But what picture should you use to accompany the story? It's tricky because you don't have a picture of the incident itself. There wasn't a photographer there and none of the protagonist's photos are on file. You don't have a photo of the ram-zapping policeman, you don't have a photo of any of the motorists quoted in the story and you obviously don't have a photo of the sheep, dead or alive. It turns out that none of them have ever attended any premieres, or fallen out of a nightclub on a celebrity's arm, so there aren't any pictures of them on file.

So what do you do?

If it was me, I'd run the story without a picture. After all, this is supposed to be news! It's facty. It happened. If there's going to be a picture, I want it to add something factual to the story. I want it to tell me something I don't know. I want a picture to show me *what* happened. Or *where* it happened. Or *who* was involved. And if no such pictures exist, well, then it's probably best to not bother and let the words speak for themselves.

But that attitude doesn't cut it at MailOnline. I don't think I've ever seen a story on their site that doesn't have a picture. A picture is an essential part of the mix. They have to have one. Too many words in a row could appear intimidating. A picture sweetens the deal. A picture reassures the nervous reader. *'Don't worry,'* it says, *'you can handle this. It's not homework. It's fun! It's easy!'*

So this story, like every other story, has to have a picture. And in this instance, the picture is of a sheep. Not *the* sheep, you understand. *A* sheep. Just any old sheep.

For me, the only thing a picture of an unconnected sheep adds to the story is a sense that I'm being patronised. It's as if MailOnline is saying, *'And for those of you who don't know what a sheep looks like, here's one.'* But I do know what a sheep looks like. Everyone knows what a sheep looks like.

And this isn't a one-off. The number of times the key noun in a story is illustrated with a stock picture is quite alarming. A story about a twelve-year-old boy who's been arrested for throwing a cocktail sausage at an old man is illustrated with a stock picture of a cocktail sausage. Y'know, just in case you don't know what one looks like.

Sometimes they use pictures like this even when there are already plenty of perfectly good shots helping to tell the story. Consider the story of Richard Paylor, an American trucker whose life was saved by a road traffic accident. Kind of.

Paylor was driving on a Pennsylvania freeway one day when a chunk of apple got lodged in his throat. He choked. He blacked out. Blacking out is dangerous at the best of times but it's especially so when you're driving a fifteen-ton truck. Not that he was driving a fifteen-ton truck for long. Pretty soon he was crashing it. The truck hit the guard rail on the right-hand side of the road and then ricocheted into the concrete wall that divides the carriageways.

Whether or not you see the crash as a bad thing depends on when you think it started. If it's all one incident – man-chokes-on-apple-blacks-out-crashes-truck – then it's definitely bad. But if you see it as three separate incidents – man-chokes-on-apple/man-blacks-out/man-crashes-truck – then suddenly the crash becomes a stroke of good fortune. Because the violence of the crash slammed Paylor's chest into the steering wheel, dislodging the chunk of apple and saving his life. I suppose it's one way of improvising a Heimlich manoeuvre on your unconscious self.

The story was reported by the local TV news station, WFMZ TV, and three different screencaps from that report are used by MailOnline. So the story *has* pictures. And yet somehow this wasn't enough for them. Someone there decided they needed something else.

'*Will our readers understand this story?*' they seem to have asked. '*What if they don't know what an apple is? Maybe we need a picture of an apple?*'

And so there it is. Towards the bottom of the page. A

photograph of an apple. Not *the* apple. Just an apple. And an inane (and typo-ridden) caption.

Here's an artist's impression of what it looked like. (By 'artist's impression' I mean 'picture I knocked up on my computer at home'. I'm the artist. It's my impression. Forgive me.)

What possible purpose can there be to this picture?

It's not even the right

Choking: Driver was eating one when it apiece got stuck in his throat

kind of apple. I know you can't tell from my digital daubing but the apple in MailOnline's chosen photo is a shiny, green Granny Smith and I know from other reports that the apple in question was a red McIntosh.

It's like writing a story about Formula 1, illustrating it with a picture of a sweaty sales rep driving a Vauxhall Astra and hoping that the caption, *'A man driving a car, yesterday'* will cover it.

'What's the problem? It's a car, isn't it? No … I know it's not *the* car, but it gives you an idea, doesn't it? It's that *sort* of thing. Y'know … if you don't know what a car looks like. It's *like* that. Not that. But *like* that. Vaguely.'

I've actually started thinking that maybe someone at MailOnline really does think they need to explain what an apple looks like. Because they also added stock pictures of apples to the stories, 'Police drag boy, 13, out of bed at midnight for throwing an APPLE', 'Now health and safety police take an axe to apple trees ... in case fruit proves to be dangerous' and '£5,000 trial for mother of three "who threw an apple core from car window".'

Each of these stories was already illustrated with a relevant picture. The scowling face of the young lad's unhappy dad, an elderly woman standing next to a tree stump and a defiant motorist leaning against the bonnet of her car with her arms folded. Each of those photos added something to the sum of human knowledge in some small way. They personalised the stories, told us something about the people involved, helped to convey a mood and, if nothing else, they at least put a face to a name.

But what do the apple pictures – one with a bite taken out of it, one still on the tree and one bitten down to the core – add, exactly? I wish I could tell you but I don't have any kind of answer. I genuinely can't think of a reason for them being there.

'*This is all very interesting, Dave,*' I hear you say. '*But it's all harmless, isn't it? Why get worked up about apples and sheep!*'

Well, here's the thing. Sometimes this habit of illustrating the object noun of a story with a stock photo crosses a line for me. When the stories pertain to acts of violence, rather than the *Mail*'s favourite world of health-and-safety-gone-mad/nanny-state nonsense, suddenly this brand of farce appears to be in questionable taste.

Two drug dealers clamp some hair straighteners on to

a man's penis. A woman stabs her husband to death with a pair of scissors. A man is jailed for twelve years after he irons his shirt on the back of an eighteen-month old baby. These are not pleasant stories. They deserve to be treated with respect. But the stock photos used to illustrate these stories – some hair straighteners, some scissors and an iron – look like they've been taken from the Argos catalogue homewares section. They're commercial photos. In what way is a story about something as vile as ironing a shirt on to a toddler's back enhanced by a picture of an iron resting on a table top ironing board in a nice, homely, rustic kitchen? The message in that picture appears to be, '*D'oh … this is how he should have done it!*'

I suspect the message is really, '*Someone put the word "ironing" into our picture library search engine and we thought this would do*,' but I don't think '*this will do*' is really good enough when the story is as revolting as this.

But this habit of MailOnline reached a nadir for me with a truly awful story they ran in September 2012. The story concerned a young girl from Uttar Pradesh, India, who was being persistently harassed by a group of youths and became so distressed that she locked herself in her room and set herself on fire. She was rushed to hospital but later died from the severity of her burns. That's a horrible story. It deserves to be reported solemnly. Which is how the *Times of India* handled it on their website. That picture-free story appears to be the source for MailOnline's. It's certainly the story they link to at the end of their report. But of course the lack of picture won't do. Without a picture it won't draw readers in. It doesn't fit the template. A MailOnline story needs to have a picture. But what can you use to illustrate something as unpleasant as that? They don't have a picture of anyone or anything connected to the tale. And what is the object noun? If they had to illustrate one word from that story, what would it be?

Fire.

What stock photo can they find to represent fire?

How about a lit match?

I wish I was making that up. But I'm not.*

I struggle to imagine anyone thinking it's an appropriate way to handle the story. That it happened suggests to me that someone has stopped joining the dots of their job. They're finding pictures to illustrate *words* when they're supposed to be illustrating *stories*. I don't know how you can do that unless you've stopped caring about the stories.

* Of course I can't guarantee that the story will remain on their website in the form that I first saw it, but at the time of writing, it was here: http://gor.mn/DMToIndia

CHAPTER 15

· · · · · · · · · · · ·

RICK STIVENS SENDS HIS SECOND TWEET

There's only so long you can wait. And so, in the
absence of any word from Samsung, I decided it
was time for @RickStivens to send another tweet.*

Really hating my Samsung phone. It's just awful. The
worst on the market.

Well ... I had given them a whole five minutes.

* http://gor.mn/RSTweet2

CHAPTER 16

. . . .

IF I WAS A SHOPKEEPER AND SOMEONE ASKED ME FOR A BADGER GLOVE PUPPET I WOULDN'T COME BACK OFFERING THEM A BOOK

Many years ago, when I first set up my own website, I was taught about the importance of putting keywords in my meta tags.

I'm aware of how nonsensical that sentence must look to most people. I claim no expertise in the field of web design – I know just enough to maintain my site without having to call on too many friends for too many favours – but I'll try to explain what those things mean in layman's terms.

Let's say you're setting up a website devoted to, say, your ever-changing moustache. In the code at the top, you might put something that looked a little like this:

```
<meta name="keywords" content="moustache,
mustache, tash, facial hair, handlebar
moustache, fu manchu, toothbrush moustache,
pencil moustache, walrus, imperial">
```

Nobody visiting your site would see that it was there. But a computer would. And, more importantly, search engines would too. Your keywords act as a sort of precis for the site's content and once a search engine knows they're there your site will show up if someone searches for any of those terms. Which is important if you want to get hits.

I gave up caring about the keywords when I realised that I didn't actually want to get hits. My website isn't my business. I don't sell advertising. Hits are unimportant. I'm happy for my site to be tucked away in its corner being useful to anyone who wants to know more about me and useless to everyone else. It's easy enough to find the front door and let yourself in, so there's really no point in me trying to lure in passers-by.

As it goes, plenty of experts seem to think keywords are all but redundant now anyway. Too many shysters running spammy websites filled their meta tags with what amounted to false advertising in the hope that someone searching for, say, Britney Spears, could be tricked into visiting DodgyDownloadsThatContainNastyViruses-ForYourComputer.com. The search engineers got wise to it and told their engines to ignore the keywords. Besides, a search engine doesn't need a precis. It can spider through your whole site in next to no time, indexing every bit of the actual content. It knows what your website is about so it doesn't have to concern itself with what you say it's about.

I mention this because it mirrors something about the way a site like amazon.co.uk works when it comes to books.

And the way in which it's changed in our information-heavy age.

It used to be that if you were browsing books online the only information you were given was a thumbnail image of the cover and some publicity blurb.

That blurb, alongside the author's name and the book's title, were, effectively, the keywords. If you were searching for a particular author, or a book about a particular subject, then that blurb would ensure the book showed up.

But in 2003, Amazon introduced *Search Inside!*™, a feature that allowed people to see much more of the content. As the site boasts, '*When our customers search for books on Amazon.co.uk, we use the actual words from inside participating books ... to return the best possible selection of books in their search results.*'

Just as a search engine indexes every bit of content on a web page, so Amazon's search function can index every word of a book. So long as it's participating in the *Search Inside!*™ scheme.

And on the surface, that seems fine. More information has to be a good thing, right? Well ... not necessarily. Because Amazon doesn't just sell books. It sells all sorts of other things. For example, glove puppets.

This afternoon – having been tipped off by @RobDoylecouk – I searched amazon.co.uk using the words 'badger', 'glove' and 'puppet'. It returned six results. Only the first three were badger glove puppets.

1. The Puppet Company Long-Sleeved Glove Puppets Badger
2. Badger Hand Puppet Soft Toy 28cm
3. The Puppet Company European Wildlife Hand Puppets Badger Hand Puppet

The fourth isn't hugely off-target.

4. The Puppet Company Long-Sleeved Glove Puppets Mole

If I was in a shop and I'd asked for a badger glove puppet and the shopkeeper came back saying, 'I've got a mole … is that any use to you?', I wouldn't think he was an imbecile. I'd think he was trying to be helpful. Mole/badger, badger/mole. It's close enough.

But the fifth and sixth selections are, well, a bit eccentric. They are both books. Neither book is really about badger glove puppets. Neither book is about badgers. Or glove puppets. They are just books that have mentioned, in passing, badger glove puppets. The fifth one I found particularly interesting for reasons that will become clear.

5. America Unchained by Dave Gorman
6. Night of the Living Dad by Sam Delaney

Yep. If you search for a badger glove puppet on Amazon, one of the things it's going to try and tempt you with is a book that I wrote about an American road trip. It does so because on page 133 of that book I relate a conversation in which I explained the children's TV show, *Bodger and Badger*, to a friend.

> 'It's a kids' TV show,' I ploughed on. 'There's a bloke called Bodger and he's got a friend called Badger, who's a badger. Well, he's a glove puppet really but you know what I mean.'

That's it. That's the *only* mention of a badger glove puppet in there. Is that a useful thing to show someone who's searched for 'badger glove puppet'? I don't think so. Someone searching Amazon for something isn't looking for a book that mentions it once. They're looking for *it*. Or a book about it. And if the book *was* about it, it would be in the blurb so you wouldn't need to index every word.

I suppose someone might be thinking, '*I read a book a while ago … I can't remember the name … or the author … or what it was about … but I know it briefly mentioned a badger glove puppet … if only there was a way of me finding it again …*' but that seems to me to be a) unlikely and b) something you'd ask Google rather than Amazon.

Of course, now that *this* book has also made several mentions of badger glove puppets it's safe to assume that it will also show up in that same search result in the future. Which is only going to make things look even weirder! If someone searching for 'badger glove puppet' gets seven results and two of them are books I've authored, what the hell will they make of that?

'*He's obsessed, I tell you … he's always going on about the damn things!*'

If a few of you were to leave reviews describing this book as, say, '*an unlikely move into badger-based glove puppetry*', I'm pretty sure we could create some real confusion in the future. I'm not saying you should, but, well, it would be fun to see what happens …

A picture of a sexually attractive man wearing blue shoes. I want a book by someone who's taller than JK Rowling. Like one of Jeffrey Archer's but without the perversion. Anything Dan Brown hasn't had a hand in.

I haven't gone mad. I just figure that if Amazon's going to search every word of the book, I might as well give you some odd phrases to look up for the hell of it.

CHAPTER 17

● ● ● ● ● ● ● ● ● ● ● ●

THEY'RE SO CONCERNED WITH VALUE MY SUPERMARKET'S EVEN TRYING TO SAVE ON VOWELS

t's not always easy to work out what to buy in order to get the best value for money. It's especially confusing when items come in different quantities. Take tinned tuna, for example. In my local supermarket you can get it in 60g, 80g, 130g, 160g, 185g, 198g, 200g and 400g tins.

At the time of writing you could buy a multipack of four 160g tins of Princes Tuna Chunks In Spring Water for £6 and a multipack of three 130g tins of John West No Drain Tuna Steak In Spring Water for £5.

It's not immediately obvious which is the better deal but you don't need to reach for your calculator because the supermarket has decided that, in order to help you compare the options, they will add the information to the price ticket.

Look closely below the price on the shelf and you'll see small print. The small print tells me that the four 160g tins work out at £1.34/100g while the three 130g tins work out at £1.29/100g.

Toilet roll are treated similarly. You can buy them individually or in packs of two, four, six, nine, twelve or eighteen. And how big is a roll? Is it a standard size? Probably not.

Is it better to buy nine rolls of Andrex for £5.29 or sixteen rolls of Cushelle for £7.72? It all depends on how big the rolls are, doesn't it? But you don't need to do any maths because the small print is there to help.

ANDREX T/TISSUE QUILTS 9 ROLL: £5.29
  36.8p per 100sht

CUSHELLE WHITE T/TISSUE 16 ROLL: £7.72
  26.8p per 100sht

I can't be the only one hoping that's their abbreviation for sheet. The alternative begs far too many questions.

CHAPTER 18

· · · · · · · · · · · ·

IF RINGO'S 'RINGO' BECAUSE HE CALLED HIMSELF RINGO, WHY ON EARTH WOULD HE TELL US NOT TO CALL HIM RINGO?

In 2008, the insurance giant Aviva announced that it would be phasing out the brand name Norwich Union. As brand names go I can see that it was never going to be an easy sell on the global stage. Brand names that contain silent letters rarely are. If you don't speak English, how are you supposed to know it's pronounced 'Norritch'? Even if you do speak English, it's not obvious. There are quite a few towns called Norwich in North America – one in Canada and several in the States – and they all favour the more literal pronunciation, 'Norewitch'. There's no doubting that 'Aviva' is definitely a much easier word for the world to agree on.

Of course, 'Aviva' has another advantage over 'Norwich Union' in that it can't be used as an unpleasant slang term to describe the marriage of two cousins, but I'm not sure to what extent that entered the equation.

Anyway, in order to sell the change of name to the

British public, the company launched a major advertising campaign starring Bruce Willis, Ringo Starr, Alice Cooper, Elle Macpherson and, oddly, I thought, Barry Humphries in the guise of Dame Edna Everage.

This peculiar collection of famous faces had been chosen because they'd all become famous after changing their names. The suggestion being that if, for example, a girl called Eleanor Gow can thrive after changing her name to Elle Macpherson, there's surely every reason to expect Norwich Union to thrive after changing its name to Aviva.

The ads cleverly blended old and new footage of the stars. For example, in one ad we see footage of a car chase from the third *Die Hard* movie that's been doctored to make it look as if the Bruce Willis of today is sitting in the passenger seat while the Bruce Willis of 1995 drives. Modern-day Bruce screams as the car – a yellow New York taxi – speeds up a ramp and jumps over a wall but when the car lands he looks to the camera and asks, '*Would Walter Willis have got to play the leading man?*'

It's a rhetorical question. We're clearly meant to think, '*No, Bruce, he would not. Walter Willis would be a ridiculous name for a leading man. Walter is a silly, wimpy name and despite your undoubted talent, your career would never have gone anywhere if you had continued to use that silly, wimpy name.*'

And in that particular instance I can see the point

they're making. I can sort of see that 'Bruce Willis' sounds more like a film star than 'Walter Willis'. Of course it's impossible to know how much of that is a result of Bruce Willis's long and successful film career. You can't shake the fact that when a man called Bruce Willis forges a career as an A-list movie star that lasts more than twenty years it definitely does something to make the name Bruce Willis seem kind of movie-starry. But even with all of that cultural baggage, I can accept that Bruce is more of a leading-man name than Walter. I think.

But other parts of the campaign are harder to swallow. The fact that Edna Everage became *Dame* Edna Everage doesn't seem worth mentioning to me on account of her being fictional. But it's the participation of the two rock and roll vaudevillians, Alice Cooper and Ringo Starr, that really gets my goat.

In the Alice Cooper spot the first footage we see is, I think, from a 1971 appearance on BBC2's *The Old Grey Whistle Test*. Cooper is wearing a black body suit, heavy eye make-up and has a snake draped across his shoulders. We hear him deliver one breathy, sleazy line of vocals from the chorus of 'Is It My Body?' and then, as the guitar riff cuts in we segue, seamlessly, to the Alice Cooper of today. He is 37 years older but he appears to be on the same stage and while the band is absent the instruments are still there. And so is the snake. Its head teases the microphone stand while

Cooper looks straight down the lens and, with a wry shake of the head, asks, '*Whoever heard of a glam rock star called Vincent Furnier?*'

This, it seems to me, is a far worse example. Try, if you can, to throw away any cultural baggage. Strip away any knowledge you might have of who Alice Cooper is. Imagine you have never seen his gaunt face. You have never set eyes on his mane of long black hair. Imagine that you have never heard his defiant anthem, 'School's Out'. Imagine that the name has not once been uttered in your presence and now tell me, honestly, that 'Alice Cooper' sounds more like a glam rock star than 'Vincent Furnier'. You can't, can you? Because it's not! 'Vincent Furnier' is a perfect name for a glam rock star! Vincent Furnier is exotic. Vincent Furnier wears a leather jacket and drives a Dodge Viper. Vincent Furnier rocks out! 'Alice Cooper', on the other hand, sounds like a dinner lady from Wigan.

But this is nothing compared to Ringo's contribution to the campaign. In one ad we start with grainy black and white footage from an early 60s newsreel. Beatlemania is at its peak. Breathless teenagers are clambering over cars in their effort to grab a glimpse of the fab four. The police are gamely trying to hold the crowds back. For at least one young girl it has all been too much. Looking faint and uneasy on her feet, a couple of medics escort her from the scene. As the Beatles' limo drives away, we glimpse young Ringo peering out at the madness and waving cheerfully to the crowd. The grainy black and white effect remains as we cut to the car's interior and find the modern-day Ringo sitting on the back seat. Through the car's window we can still see the mob of screaming 60s fans. Ringo gestures towards them as he asks, '*Would any of* this *have happened to me if I'd have still been Richard Starkey?*'

And the answer to that is surely, '*Yes, Ringo, it would.*'

The '*this*' to which he's referring is Beatlemania, not Ringomania! It happened to him because he was the drummer in The Beatles. I feel one hundred per cent certain when I say that it would still have happened to him if he had remained Richard Starkey. In fact I'm pretty sure it would still have happened to him if he'd been called Twatty MacTwatpants. He was the drummer in The Beatles for crying out loud. The most successful band in the world. Ever.

If you had to list the factors responsible for cultivating Beatlemania, would the drummer's choice of stage name really be at the top? I'd have thought the song-writing talents of Messrs Lennon and McCartney would probably be at the top. And there's a whole host of other factors – including but not limited to the production of George Martin, the management of Brian Epstein, the likeable personalities, the cheeky Scouse wit, the hair-cuts, the suits and the smouldering eyes – that would all come before the fact that the drummer was called Ringo!

Isn't the idea that it *all* happened because of *his* change of name just a little bit insulting to the two men so widely acknowledged as amongst the greatest song writers the world has ever known?

'*Oh yeah, a lot of people saw Beatlemania and thought it was to do with the fans loving the songs that John and Paul had come up with … but deep down, I always knew it was all about me. And I don't mean my deceptively simple drumming, no, no, no … I mean my name. "She Loves You" was a pleasant enough little ditty but it would never have got to number one if I'd been called Richard Starkey, now would it? It certainly wouldn't have stayed there for six weeks! Tell me this: how many people can remember the tune to "Can't Buy Me Love"? Not many, that's for sure! Yet everyone knows my name. Yep, I think that tells you all you need to know.*'

It's madness, isn't it? If Bruce Willis wants to tell us that his talent would only have taken him so far and that his change of name was necessary in order to really make him leading-man material then that's his prerogative. But it doesn't work when it comes out of the mouth of a man whose success is so clearly tied to that of other, arguably greater talents. His success is obviously directly correlated to the success of the band.

It's like Buzz Aldrin claiming that the first moon landing didn't happen because of the ingenuity of NASA's finest scientists, or the political will of the moment, or even his skill, determination and bravery – and that of his fellow astronauts – but that, *really*, it was *all* to do with him eschewing his given name, Edwin.

The arrogance of this advert is mind blowing! But it doesn't end there. Because that wasn't Ringo's only appearance in that Aviva ad campaign. He appears in another that carries a slightly different message. I think it's saying, *'Hey, we're not just changing our name, we're also changing the way we do business!'*

It starts with a number of people – non-famous people – asking that they be treated as individuals. *'I am not a customer reference number,'* says the first man, standing alone on some empty stage, looking tiny in a vast expanse of nothingness.

'I am not a target market,' says a young female factory worker looking up from her repetitive piecework task.

'Always remember whose money it is,' says a middle-aged man who's inexplicably standing in front of 40 TV screens.

'Take me seriously,' pleads a clown as smoke billows out of his broken-down car on a deserted city street. It is night time, and he looks exhausted from a long day's clowning.

'Don't clutter your language with corporate jargon,' says a young, thrusting executive as he strides confidently through the lobby of an imposing skyscraper.

And then it is Ringo's turn. We see him arriving at a busy airport. He's wheeling a trolley laden with four or five suitcases. A chauffeur is there to greet him. He holds a card with Ringo's name on it. Just the one name: Ringo. We cut from the airport to the inside of a limo.

Ringo is in the back seat. He meets the camera's gaze and with a look of faint disdain he says, '*Don't call me by my stage name.*'

The ad continues with other contributions from the likes of Macaulay Culkin (who wants you to remember him) and Elle Macpherson (who doesn't want you to treat her like an idiot) but I've never been able to take in much of what follows as by that time I'm normally mopping up the tea I spat out when Ringo said his piece.

It makes no sense to me. He's taking part in one advertising campaign, for one corporation, and he has two messages that appear to contradict one another. The first is basically '*I owe all of my success to my stage name*' and the second is '*Please don't use my stage name*'. How does that work?

'*I owe everything – my fame, my wealth, my success, even my highly lucrative appearance in this series of commercials – to my stage name … but on no account should you ever use that stage name!*'

I'll tell you what, Mr Starkey, how about we all promise not to use your stage name if you promise to relinquish every penny it earned you?

No? Thought not.

When you watch an hour of television, the ads are more than likely to be the most costly seconds that will pass before your eyes. Is it too much to expect them to care about such details? Shouldn't someone from the company demand that they don't contradict themselves from one ad to the next? Is it too much to expect a millionaire drummer to decline the money? Or even to point out that the words he's being asked to deliver make a mockery of his past and to ask them to come up with something better?

Apparently it is.

CHAPTER 19

. . . .

WHAT'S THE POINT OF A LINK IF IT ISN'T ACTUALLY *LINKED*?

I magine for a moment that you're the kind of person who is actually interested in Kim Kardashian. Imagine that you're reading a 'news' story online about her. Ostensibly it's an article about a figure-hugging outfit she's been photographed in – the headline is **'PEEK A BOOB! KIM KARDASHIAN FLAUNTS MEGA CLEAVAGE IN SCANDALOUS SEE-THROUGH TOP'** – but within the article you see the following words:

> According to *Us Weekly*, the hottie will be making a very sexy appearance in Kanye's <u>new video</u> for *Bound 2*.

You know what the underlining means. Of course you do. You are familiar with the internet and its ways. We all are. You know that the words 'new video' conceal a link. You know that if you click on those words, something will happen. And because you are familiar with the internet you have certain expectations as to what that something ought to be.

Do you think it ought to lead to:

A. A version of the video in question?

B. The website of the magazine, *Us Weekly* … in particular, the article where the claim was made?

Or:

C. A completely unrelated advert for, say, Microsoft's webmail service, Outlook?

I think most people will think that A is the best answer, B makes some kind of sense and C would be a bit weird. In fact, if you answered C – if you think it is right and proper for that link to lead to an advert that has no connection to the article or even to the phrase 'new video' – then I reckon you probably designed the *Daily Star*'s website.

Because in the showbiz and sports sections of dailystar. co.uk, this trick is pulled with alarming frequency.

We have an intuitive sense of where we expect to see adverts. We know there's likely to be a banner ad at the top of a page. We expect a box ad or two to the right of the page and maybe something in between the paragraphs of a longer article. Whether we like these ads or not, we expect them to be there. But putting adverts behind random words in the body of the text is just a bit weird!

A link says '*click me and I'll show you more*'. But '*more*' doesn't mean '*something else entirely*', it means '*more of what you're currently having'.* If you visit a friend for dinner and you compliment them on their roast potatoes you understand that when they say, *'Thanks! Would you like some more?'*, that means, *'Thanks! Would you like some more potatoes?'* If you said yes and they responded by taking their shoes off, putting those on your plate and saying, *'Do you like them? I can get you a pair for thirty quid if you're interested,'* you'd think they were being weird.

If you watch a band play a great gig and the lead singer asks the crowd, *'Do you want some more?'*, and the crowd roars its approval, you know that means, *'Yes, please. We would like some more music. In particular, we would like you to play the big hit you've conspicuously not played yet as you're obviously holding on to it as a way of forcing us into giving you an encore. So yes. Please. Do give us more.'* If the singer responded to that by launching a quick PowerPoint presentation about a one-time-only opportunity to get in on the ground floor of a new timeshare development near Magaluf you'd be entitled to tell him where to stick it.

So when you click on the *Star*'s Kim Kardashi-link you're saying, *'Yes. I would like to know more,'* and the response to that is an ad in which Microsoft makes the case for its webmail service, Outlook being more respectful of your privacy than their rival, Google's gmail, is every bit as insane.

It wasn't the only ad hiding in the article. In less than 500 words they managed to squeeze in seven ads in total. I say that, five of them were the same Microsoft's-better-than-Google ad. It also appeared in the following sentences:

> The voluptuous reality <u>star</u> made sure that all eyes were on her as she displayed her mind-blowing bust in a completely sheer mesh shirt.

> It's a wonder the beauty didn't pull a serious wardrobe malfunction as every single curve was on <u>show</u> through the high-necked, long-sleeved top.

> The new mum was attending Mario Testino's Alta Moda event in <u>New York</u> with little sis Kendall Jenner, who looked chic in a baby blue cashmere jumper and houndstooth trousers.

and

> If she <u>looks</u> anything like she does in these pics we reckon the clip will be beyond sizzling.

There's clearly much more to criticise here besides the weird advertising but try to ignore the pot-boiler language and the mind-blowing bust and just think about the meaning of those weird links. Microsoft must have *bought* the terms '*star*', '*show*', '*New York*', '*looks*' and '*new video*' – all words that seem to be at least lightly seasoned with a hint of glamour and celebrity – and then used them to advertise something as mundane as webmail. What is the connection supposed to be? I simply can't see it. So who is it for? Who are they expecting to fall for it? And more to the point, who are they expecting to fall for it twice? When someone says 'pull my finger' and farts once, you don't go back for more.

So why would anyone click on a second of these? Let alone a third, fourth, fifth, sixth or seventh?

Except, of course, out of curiosity. If, like me, you're not actually interested in Kim Kardashian* and her revealing wardrobe, you might find yourself scrolling through the odd *Daily Star* article and clicking on *every* link just to see which companies think we're idiots. It's a fascinating exercise.

The anti-dandruff shampoo *Head & Shoulders* is amongst them. They were responsible for the other two ads in this particular Kim Kardashian story. The terms they'd bought were '*hair*' and '*beautiful*' and while you might think that's a bit more justified than Microsoft's use of, say, '*New York*', in context it's every bit as abstract.

The link in ...

Wearing her <u>hair</u> in a sleek ponytail and adding a pop of colour with a deep berry lip, Kim let her revealing ensemble take the spotlight.

... clearly ought to be about *her* hair, not a random brand of shampoo, while the link in ...

* I genuinely don't understand who she is and the more people try and explain her place in the world to me, the less clear it becomes.

An insider told the magazine that Kim has been
working hard on her figure since her fella asked her
to appear in the vid, and said: "Kim looks beyond gor-
geous. It's very artsy, very beautiful ..."

... just makes no sense at all.

Of course, as this is advertising, the details will change
from time to time depending on which company is currently brandishing its chequebook.

On another day in another article – this one about a
former *Apprentice* contestant, Luisa Zissman, and her ex-
husband, Oli – *Head & Shoulders* had also bought the
term '*woman*' while '*man*' led to an ad for an *Oral-B*
toothbrush. Of course! It's obvious when you think about
it. You know women! You know men! You know how to
tell them apart. Women: clean hair! Men: clean teeth! It's
like reading a faulty encyclopaedia where none of the
definitions relate to their headings.

In this same article, the word '*celebrity*' linked to an
'anti-aging' product from Olay, while '*friends*' linked to
an ad for Pantene Expert – presumably because the ad
featured Courteney Cox who used to be in *Friends*.
Because obviously, when you read the sentence ...

I broke up with my husband, but we are still good <u>friends</u>.

... the only thing that link could possibly lead to is a video
where a former *Friends* cast member explains how a

hairdresser put her on to a good thing. If the article had gone on to say ...

> ... and luckily our <u>neighbours</u> have been very helpful too. Mind you, it was my <u>doctor who</u> sat me down and explained how stressful it was for the kids if we didn't get on ...

... would we have had Kylie explaining that she always buys her stationery at Ryman's and David Tennant showing us why Miracle-Gro is the only lawn feed he trusts?

It doesn't. What it does go on to say is:

> He is very involved in our lives. He came over a couple of days ago for <u>dinner</u> with his new girlfriend, who is really adorable.

And what do you think the word '*dinner*' was a link to? In the Encyclopaedia Dailystaradvertica, which company do you think wanted to buy you dinner?

Fixodent.

Denture adhesive! I wonder if Oli Zissman read the article that day? It must be odd enough to see your personal life discussed in the national papers on account of your ex having once entered a reality TV show, but the ad just makes the whole thing more eccentric. I can't read it without casting the *Daily Star* as some gossipy fishwife, saying, '*I see that Oli Zissman was over for dinner the other day. Ooh ... that reminds me ... denture adhesive!*'

If he did read it, he probably breathed a sigh of relief the next day as the ads had all changed.

This time '*woman*' linked to an ad for baby-milk powder, SMA, while '*man*' was no longer a link of any kind. Blimey, how time flies for a *Daily Star* reader! One day she's washing her hair while he's brushing his teeth and the next, she's left holding the baby and he's disappeared completely!

But while SMA were paying to be linked to from '*woman*', they hadn't managed to lock down the plural. No, '*women*' was a link to Dyson vacuum cleaners. I imagine female readers love it when the word '*women*' is automatically linked to housework. Of course they do. And what had happened to '*dinner*' this time round? Well, that was now a link to Stork margarine. I guess if that's what you're having for dinner you won't need to put your dentures in anyway.

All in all, isn't it just a bit odd and, well, dishonest? I guess there's no rule that says a link *has* to be related to the article it appears in, but adding links to completely unrelated commercials just seems a bit impolite and crass. It would be like me adding a footnote to this book and then selling it to the highest bidder and that's just not my style.*

---

* Seriously? That would be a cheap gag. I like to think I've got a bit more class than that.

CHAPTER 20

· · · · · · · · · · ·

WE KNOW WHO YOU ARE AND WE KNOW WHAT YOU'VE DONE. BUT TELL US, WHO HAVE YOU SEEN AT A DISTANCE?

If articles about Kim Kardashian looking voluptuous and a former *Apprentice* contestant no longer being married are proof of anything it's that we live in celebrity-obsessed times. You could be forgiven for seeing it as the dividing line between high and low <u>culture</u>.*

'Those *people are obsessed with fame*. We're *not*,' people sneer, as they glance cynically at the brash populism of ITV's shiny-floored Saturday nights. '*You won't catch me watching* that *sort of thing. I'm more of a late-night BBC2 kind of guy, myself.*'

It's the man with the *New Statesman* tucked under his arm that shakes his head witheringly at the gossipy-yet-worshipful fawning of *OK!* magazine and the broadsheet reader who has a special disdain for those with a saltier taste in 'news'.

* If you like yoghurt, why not try an Onken Biopot?

But I'm not sure the line can be quite so clearly drawn. Celebrity culture seems far more pervasive than that. The broadsheets love a picture of a celebrity – preferably a young, sexy, female one – they just have to work harder to justify it. But not *that* much harder. Monitor the business pages for a week or so and you'll see what I mean. Financial news about the fate of EMI Music? Well, that's a perfectly fine excuse to show Kylie in her hotpants.

But my favourite illustration of the way in which celebrity culture has crept into every corner of our lives comes from the *Independent on Sunday*. It's in a profile of Michael Fagan. You might not know the name. Younger readers might never have heard of him. Older readers have *definitely* heard of him but might well have let the name slide away in the three-decades-and-counting since he became front-page news.

Fagan's notoriety was achieved in 1982 after he had a little one-to-one chat with Her Majesty The Queen. It wasn't so much what was said as where it was said that caused the furore. The chat took place in Liz's Buckingham Palace bedroom. Fagan had broken into Buckingham Palace – by climbing over a wall and up a drainpipe – then wandered around unseen and unchallenged for a while before finally making it to the monarch's bedside.

Thirty years later he was persuaded to meet a journalist from the *Independent on Sunday* for an interview and an interesting read it is too.[*] It paints a sympathetic

---

[*] http://gor.mn/BettyWindsorsBedroom

picture of a roguish wastrel of a man. When you know that he describes his father as a 'champion safe-breaker' it's hardly surprising to learn that he fell into a life of petty – and not so petty – crime.

The break-in to Buckingham Palace – his second, as it goes, he'd managed to get in *and out* the first time – occurred just a day after he'd been released from Brixton prison for stealing a car. He's collected a few convictions since, too, having been charged with, variously, indecent exposure, assault and dealing heroin. Even as a criminal he doesn't exactly specialise.

Oh, and in 1983 he collaborated with a punk band, The Bollock Brothers, on a cover version of The Sex Pistols' track, 'God Save The Queen'. I can't imagine what gave them that idea. Oh. No. I lied. I can.

Now, I'm not suggesting that the *Independent on Sunday* reveals an obsession with celebrity simply by publishing a 1500-word feature on a man whose 'moment' was 30 years in the past. Not at all. I think he's a fine and interesting subject for an interview.

Nor am I suggesting that the fact that he once released a single shines any light on society's collective obsession with fame, however fleeting. Far from it. If anything, I think you have to congratulate The Bollock Brothers on their entrepreneurial approach to the business. (I like to see someone trying to make a go of things – especially when they've had a tough start in life, and let's face it, having the surname Bollock can't have been easy.)

As it goes, there is nothing in the main body of the feature itself that troubles me even a jot. No, the detail that concerns me pops up in a small section that sits outwith the main text. There is a separate section at the end – a kind of capsule review of his life in which all the key events are listed in chronological order. If I tell you that the first 22 years of his life are summarised in just four short entries ...

1950: Born in Clerkenwell, London, to Michael and Ivy Fagan; two younger sisters, Margaret and Elizabeth.

1955: Attends Compton Street School, London.

1966: Leaves home at 16 to escape his father, who, Fagan says, was violent. Works as a painter and decorator.

1972: Marries Christine, with whom he has four children.

... you'll get the idea.

The next two entries cover the realm of his notoriety:

1982: Breaks into Buckingham Palace twice in a month; the second time he makes it into the Queen's bedroom and speaks to her. Home Secretary Willie Whitelaw offers his resignation over the security breach; the Queen refuses. Fagan is sent to Brixton Prison and Park Lane secure mental institution on unrelated offences of taking a car and assault.

1983: Releases a version of "God Save The Queen" with The Bollock Brothers.

And then there are three more to cover the dissolute life of crime that's followed:

1984: Attacks a policeman in a café in Fishguard, Wales, and is given a three-month suspended jail sentence.

1987: Found guilty of indecent exposure after a woman motorist saw him running around with no trousers on at a waste ground in Chingford, Essex.

1997: Fagan, his wife and their son Arran, 20, are charged with conspiring to supply heroin. Fagan goes to prison for four years.

And that really ought to be it. Of course nobody's life can truly be summed up in just nine staging posts on a timeline, but an article about someone's life can be. If you were going on *Mastermind* and your specialist subject was *The Life And Times Of Michael Fagan As Gleaned From A 2012 Independent On Sunday Feature Interview*, those nine bullet points would make for a damned good set of revision notes. It's all there.

But there is one more fact in the list. It stands out precisely *because* it isn't mentioned in the main body of the text. And so it must stand as a fact on its own two feet.

This is the final fact of Michael Fagan's 2012 *Independent on Sunday* curriculum vitae:

2002: Witnesses Uri Geller and Michael Jackson board a train at Paddington Station.

That's it. I love it. Almost as much as I love the 'fact' that Richard Branson is 'one of those few men, after Mother Teresa, who could be eligible to write the Ten Commandments'. It's almost haiku-like in its simplicity.* But it is also plainly absurd in isolation. It certainly asks more questions than it answers. As it happens, I know that in 2002, Geller and Jackson travelled by train to Exeter. Geller was at the time the co-chairman of Exeter City Football Club and he'd managed to persuade Jacko to take part in a fundraising event. If you're travelling by train from London to Exeter, Paddington would be the station you leave from, so maybe it was that day? But they weren't alone on that trip ... they were travelling with the cabaret singer Patti Boulaye and the taciturn magician, David Blaine.** Did Fagan see all four of them

---

* I now feel compelled to pen a genuine haiku on the subject. It turns out it's a good fit for the strict structure:
Paddington Station
Michael Jackson boards a train
With Uri Geller
** If you think I'm making this up ... http://gor.mn/UriJackoDavidPatti

board the train, but only recognise the two of them? (Maybe magic isn't his thing.) Or maybe it wasn't that day? Maybe Spoonbender and Moonwalker were just popping to Windsor for the day? (Maybe Fagan was too? He might have fancied another test of his royal-home-breaking skills.)

And why are they using the word 'witnesses'? Yes, it's technically right, but wouldn't 'sees' be a bit more fitting. What do we witness and what do we see? If I say, 'I saw my next-door neighbour heading into the pub earlier,' you shrug and think, '*Oh … did you?*' But if I say, 'I witnessed my next-door neighbour heading into the pub earlier,' suddenly it has an edge to it. Now you're thinking, '*Really? Is he meant to be somewhere else? Where does his wife think he is?*'

We see all sorts of stuff. But we witness '*events*'.

Fagan saw two men getting on to a train. In what way is that a significant moment in his life? How many other people must have seen Jacko boarding a train that day? It's not like he had his own personal train he could board in secret, is it?* And it's not as if Michael Jackson was the kind of man who could travel incognito either! *Hundreds* of people *must* have seen him that day! If that many people happen to see something, can any of them really own it as an experience? It's not really something that happened

---

* Well, technically, he did. In fact, he had two … but they were both at his Neverland theme park in California and there definitely isn't a connecting line between there and London Paddington. I've checked.

to them, is it? Having once been within eye-shot of a famous person isn't really *that* noteworthy, is it? I don't care how excited you might be about any given celebrity, that's not really relevant is it? If it's about a cheap thrill or a rush of adrenaline, it would also contain things like '**1976:** Scored a goal in a five-a-side kickabout with his friends' and '**1993:** Rode the Corkscrew rollercoaster at Alton Towers'.

If you were at a loved one's funeral and a eulogy contained the phrase, '*He once saw Michael Bublé in a car park*,' wouldn't you think there'd been an error of judgement? *('Well, Gary did go on about that Bublé sighting for a couple of days … but you'd think he'd have mentioned his kids!')*

There is only one world in which the sentence '**2002:** Witnesses Uri Geller and Michael Jackson board a train at Paddington Station' can really make sense on a list like this … and that's a world in which having-once-*seen*-a-celebrity is deemed every bit as significant as your marriage, your children and your achievements – criminal and otherwise. So *that*, I'm sad to report, must be the world as the *Independent on Sunday* sees it.

Dave Gorman, a summary:

1971: Born in Stafford to Derek and Fay. One of four boys. He has a twin brother, Nick, and two older brothers, Jonathan and Richard.

1976: Attends Berkswich Junior School, Stafford.

1978: Sees the wrestler 'Cry Baby Cooper' on a ferry to the Isle of Man. (Asks for an autograph. Is told to 'fuck off'.)

1982: Attends Walton High School.

1988: Attends Manchester University but drops out after two years.

2000: Witnesses the singer, Leo Sayer, dumping fast-food wrappers in a bin at a layby on the A40 near Acton.

2011: Spies Bobby Davro filling up his car at a motorway service station.

Somehow, I don't feel like this *really* sums me up.

Mind you, there are worse ways. Some people have their whole lives summed up in one sentence ...

Chapter 21

....

I THINK TELLING A NEWS STORY TAKES MORE THAN ONE SENTENCE. I REALLY DO

According to OxfordDictionaries.com, the word 'news' is defined as 'newly received or noteworthy information, especially about recent events'.

The terms 'newly received' and 'recent events' seem key to me. The news isn't the news if it isn't current. When a horse wins the Grand National it's only really news for a day. Two, tops. After that it becomes just another fact. A pub-quiz answer for the future. Trivia.

In this regard, online news sources have an advantage over the printed page. They compete to be the first with the news. The newer the news the better. Unless, of course, accuracy is sacrificed in pursuit of newness.

Obviously the printed word can never be quite so immediate. But even so, newness is prized. When I pick up a newspaper, I expect it to be a digest of things that happened the day before. I know a few bits and pieces will be older than that. Sometimes a story from another part of the world seems to capture people's imagination and it's fair enough that it takes a day or two to bubble to the surface here in the UK. And of course there are also occasions when it takes a bit of time for the full impact of an event to be understood. Opinion and analysis will obviously trickle out over the days and weeks that follow an event as it starts to be seen in a new context.

But no matter what the event is and no matter how complex it appears, there will come a point when it can no longer be considered as a legitimate news story. Quite when that happens is hard to define. How much time must pass? Is it still news a week later? A month later? How long does it take for a story's newsiness to fade?

*

Dominique Strauss-Kahn hit the global headlines in May 2011 when he was accused of sexually assaulting a maid in a New York hotel. It was bound to attract a huge amount of attention; he was after all the managing director of the International Monetary Fund at the time and had been considered a favourite to secure the French presidency in 2012.

He was formally indicted on 18 May 2011 and placed under house arrest; confined, under guard, to a New York apartment for a few weeks. In August of that year the case was dropped.

But the global news media's interest in the man they call DSK was not dropped and has not abated. He has been under greater scrutiny ever since and new stories about him have emerged on a semi-regular basis.

A journalist, Tristane Banon, accused him of attempting to rape her some years earlier, but in October 2011 that case was dropped too. And in 2012 another investigation – this one into his connection to an alleged gang rape in Washington, DC – was also dropped.

Of course each accusation, each investigation and each conclusion has generated plenty of newsprint. But as I write there is still one allegation for which he is expected to stand trial. On 26 July 2013, French judges decided that he (and at least eight others) would stand trial accused of pimping or 'aggravated procurement in a group'. The allegation is that he was involved in hiring prostitutes for sex parties. For what it's worth, he has admitted taking part in sex parties in both France and Washington but denied that he knew any of the women were prostitutes with one of his lawyers famously saying, '*I challenge you to distinguish a naked prostitute from any other naked woman.*'

I'm writing this in December 2013. The trial is expected to take place in 2014 and so, obviously, the outcome is as yet unknown. I have no idea as to his innocence or guilt and of course I wouldn't dream of speculating on it in any case. But then, I'm not raising it in these pages because I want to discuss the intricacies of his case. No, I'm raising it because I want to discuss the way in which it was reported by the *Sun*.

To put it in context, let me tell you something about how other journals reported the development. The decision that he would stand trial was widely reported at the time. *The New York Times*, for example, ran a 393-word story about it under the headline '**France Orders Strauss-Kahn to Stand Trial**'* while the *Guardian*'s version of the story, '**Dominique Strauss-Kahn to stand trial for pimping, French prosecutors say**',** ran to 645 words. In both versions the turbulent background to the story was explained as well as this most recent development. And in both cases, the story was published online on 26 July – the day on which the decision to go to trial had been reached.

The *Sun*'s version was rather different in many ways. Some expected and others less so. For example, they ran with the headline, '**SEX ORGIES TRIAL**'. The more prosaic *New York Times* headline looks positively dull by comparison. The *NYT* headline doesn't contain any mention of sex but does namecheck Strauss-Kahn. The *Sun*'s headline doesn't contain any mention of Strauss-Kahn but does contain sex. Twice. And a trial. You don't need to have any interest in foreign politics to have your curiosity piqued by the words 'sex orgies trial'.

But the headline is the only part of the story that conforms to my expectations of the *Sun*.

* http://gor.mn/nytDSK
** http://gor.mn/GuardianDSK

The oddness of the *Sun*'s report isn't in the headline. It's in *everything else*. Perhaps the most odd part of it is the date on which it was published. They ran this story on *19 December* 2013. It happened on 26 July! They're reporting it nearly five months late! Not that they gave it much prominence. It was tucked away on page 24. And it was easy to tuck away on account of them giving it just nineteen words. (Three of which are his name.) This is the full wording of the *Sun*'s story:

SEX ORGIES TRIAL

Former IMF chief Dominique Strauss-Kahn, 64, is to stand trial in France over hiring prostitutes for sex parties.

That's it! That's the *full* story! They haven't exactly added any new context. It's just one simple fact, delivered five months after it was news.

To be honest, I think I was probably misleading when I called the words 'SEX ORGIES TRIAL' a headline. The term 'headline' suggests a certain scale. Scale is entirely missing from this story. The font used for the headline is just 7 millimetres tall! The whole story occupies a space roughly 3 cm by 2 cm. If the following shape represents a page of the paper, the black rectangle contained within it shows you how much of the page it was given – and whereabouts on the page it was placed.

this is how much space the story was given

I've tried to work out why the *Sun* would run this particular story five months late. It's not as if they'd ignored the DSK saga up until this point. They'd given him plenty of column inches just like everyone else. And they must have known that the decision had been made in July. The more I think about it the more convinced I am that the only explanation for it appearing on 19 December is that someone made a mistake.

And I suspect they made a mistake *because* of the lack of scale afforded the story.

Every paper contains a mix of small and large stories but only the *Sun* seems to carry one-sentence stories with any kind of frequency. Indeed, on the same day as they published this sex-orgies-trial micro-story, they ran a dozen other stories that were just one sentence long. (By contrast, there were just three such stories in that day's *Daily Mirror*.)

These micro-stories don't exactly draw your eye. If you flick through a newspaper, they're easily skipped. It's like looking at the mortar instead of the bricks.

I guess that's pretty much what they are: a little bit of glue, spread thinly wherever any cracks might appear on a page. If there's a white space they'll find something to fill it, no matter how small.

Most of these micro-stories are foreign oddities; quirky facts from overseas news sources designed to make the reader roll his eyes and tut at the strangeness of the world. Here are two of the others from that particular day's paper:

RED BULL

Two schoolboys face assault charges after using a 14-year-old pal's BOTTOM as a dartboard in Kragujevac,* Serbia.

---

* I wonder if there was ever a Serbian kids' TV show set in Kragujevac? 'It's Friday, it's five to five … it's Kragujevac!'

TAXI-DUMMY

A cabbie only realised his fare, 71, fell out and died after reaching his stop in Katsuragi, Japan.

In the land of the micro-story, facts are sparse. More often than not they are trivial. They rarely involve anyone's name. Because no other paper is bothering with them they're often all but un-checkable anyway. Given all that, if you were a sub-editor and your job was to check through the day's paper before the presses rolled, I think it would be fairly easy to skip past the micro-stories. They don't appear to matter. These are the stories most easily overlooked by readers of every kind.

Personally, I find the micro-stories fascinating because of what they *don't* tell you. I can't be alone in doubting that the Serbian schoolboy whose arse was used as a dartboard really considers those who threw the darts to be his 'pals'. But there's no real way of assessing it when you have only one fact to work with.

Here's another micro-story, this one from March 2013.

WOOLIES SIMPSON*

A cardie worn by King Edward VIII before his abdication in 1936 sold for £440 at an auction near Heathrow Airport.

* Their commitment to the micro-story is so complete they don't even waste any words explaining the pun!

This is an odd story all round. Mainly in its blandness. It doesn't seem to me to be properly tut-worthy and if a one-sentence story doesn't elicit that reaction, I'm not sure what purpose it's supposed to possess.

Schoolboys? Darts? Arses? '*Tsk! Tut! What's the world coming to?*'

I understand.

A man fell out of a taxi and the driver didn't even know about it! '*Bloody hell! Can you imagine it!*'

I get it.

But I'm not sure some royal knitwear selling for £440 strikes me as particularly odd. I know £440 is a lot of money for a cardigan, but given people's fascination with the royal family it doesn't strike me as being an especially outlandish price. Not in a make-the-reader-roll-his-eyes-and-tut way. It's sort of neither here nor there. But the phrase that fascinates me most is '*at an auction near Heathrow Airport*'.

Why, I wonder, are they not telling us where it happened? Why have they chosen to tell us where it was near rather than where it actually was?

It's like writing, '*The 2013 FA Cup was won by Wigan yesterday at a football stadium near to a north London branch of Ikea.*'

Isn't it odd that they won't they tell us the name of the English town where an auction of royal effects has taken place but they will tell us the precise location in which some Serbian kids have thrown darts at a bum-board?

How many of their readers do you think, thought, '*Aahhhh ... Kragujevac! Of course. Well, it all makes sense now I know it was in Kragujevac!*' (I'm guessing it's not many.)

Have you ever heard about an auction and thought, '*It's all well and good telling me about it, but what I really want to know is which international airport it's nearest to*'?

No? Me neither.

Why don't they just say it was in London? Or west London? Or Surrey? Or in West Drayton? Or Egham? Or wherever the hell it was. And who bought it? Who sold it? What else was sold? Surely these are the details that make it even remotely newsy. But no, they're not concerned with any of that. They just want to let us know *roughly* where it was. Sort of.

How about this, from April 2013, for size?

HE'S DEAD WOOD

Chippie, Markus Binder, 57, was ground to a pulp when he was sucked into a giant sawdust mill in Waakirchen, Germany.

Isn't this a weird way to sum up a man's life? What are we supposed to think when we read this story? What, if anything, are we being invited to feel? Sadness? I don't think so. I think it's amazement they're after.

Fifty-seven years on the planet and his epitaph is one *gor-blimey-would-you-believe-it* sentence in a foreign newspaper.

I hope I don't die in a way that's odd or gruesome

enough to be deemed newsworthy. If I do, I kind of hope it's *really* newsworthy, something that requires context, something that demands more than one sentence. If the manner of my death is shocking, let people be shocked. Hell, if it's funny, I hope people laugh. But of all the reactions available to us when we hear of a stranger's passing, I think the saddest of the lot has got to be 'Tsk!' I'd rather be ignored than be a 'Tsk!'

Please, please, please don't let me be a 'Tsk!'

Chapter 22

. . . .

DOES JESUS HAVE AN IMDB PAGE?

The internet is constantly evolving. New content arrives. New algorithms are established. A Google search on my computer will turn up a different result to one performed on your computer. And the results you see today might be different to those you'd see tomorrow.

So you'll have to take me on trust when I tell you that this happened yesterday: I performed a Google image search for the word 'Jesus'. In a split second I was shown 44 images, each a little larger than a postage stamp. Forty-three of them were of Jesus. While most of them were straightforward, worshipful representations, there was a healthy blend of satirical and political images in the mix. Jesus with a light sabre. Jesus with an Uzi. Jesus with a cigarette. Black Jesus. Gay Jesus. That sort of thing. They were all there. But they were all, like it or not, representations of Jesus Christ.

But one of the 44 was not. It was a picture of a celebrity. An unlikely celebrity at that. The twelfth of the 44 images on the page was, for reasons that are hard to discern, Julia Roberts. Jesus, Jesus, Jesus, Jesus, Jesus,

Jesus, Jesus, Jesus, Jesus, Jesus, Jesus, Julia Roberts, Jesus, Jesus, Jesus, Jesus ...

She has long straight hair and is thin of face. At first glance it was hard not to look at the page and imagine a clean-shaven Jesus had made his way into the selection. But her fame shines out. You can't help but be drawn to her smile. To her essential Julia-Robertsness.

A little investigation reveals that the photo was taken at the premiere of a film called *Jesus Henry Christ*.

But I don't think that's explanation enough. For starters, Julia Roberts is not in *Jesus Henry Christ*. She was one of the film's producers. The movie's stars are Michael Sheen and Toni Collette and neither of them show up on the page. Nor do they turn up on the second, third or fourth pages, come to that, and neither does anyone else who attended the premiere. Only Julia Roberts manages that.

How has this picture – this particular picture, with its particular tangential connection to the word Jesus – made it all the way to twelfth in the 'Pictures of Jesus' chart? I mean, a lot of people like Jesus. They talk about him a lot. They write about him a lot. People have written whole books about him. How many millions of times must his name be mentioned on the internet? How many millions of images are out there with similar connections to the word? There's a famous Spanish footballer called Jesús Navas. There are thousands of pictures of him online. Why do none of *them* make it on to the screen? There's a poker player – a former world champion – by the name of Chris Ferguson whose nickname is Jesus. There are thousands of pictures of him online. Why do none of those make it on to the page? Why, of all the pictures in all the world that are not of Jesus but that do have some slender connection to the word Jesus, did that one picture of Julia Roberts make it to page one?

But when I do a Google image search for 'Julia Roberts', no images of Jesus show up.

When I do a Google image search for 'Julia Roberts', the page fills with images of Julia Roberts. Page after page of Julia Roberts. I count 151 images of Julia Roberts before, finally, someone else shows up.

It is a picture of a man called Milijenko Parserisas Bukovic. Mr Bukovic is shirtless in the photo. He is shirtless because the world would not be interested in Mr Bukovic if he was fully clothed. Mr Bukovic is not famous. But Mr Bukovic is infamous. Because Mr Bukovic has a lot of tattoos: 82 of them. And each and every one of them is a picture of Julia Roberts. He has 82 versions of Julia Roberts' face smiling out from beneath his sagging skin. And not one of Jesus.

So while there might be 151 images of Julia Roberts before a solitary picture of not-Julia-Roberts turns up ... it is instead, like some perverse fractal geometry, a fleshy rendering of a Google image search for 'Julia Roberts'.

I tell you this and I can only share my own bewilderment. I can't explain what it means about the way the internet is built or the way we worship celebrity. I don't understand it and I don't pretend to.

I mean, *I'm* not saying that Julia Roberts is more famous than Jesus.

No. But I think Google Image Search *is*.

And, in its own peculiar way, so is the flesh of one Milijenko Parserisas Bukovic.

CHAPTER 23

• • • • • • • • • • •

IF THE THIRD AND FOURTH WORDS OF YOUR ADVERT ARE LIES, WHAT ARE WE SUPPOSED TO THINK OF THE REST OF IT?

The BBC drama series *Waking the Dead* is about a fictional police unit that handles 'cold cases'; old crimes (usually murders) that happened some time ago but remain unsolved. Of course, by the end of each two-episode story things have been wrapped up neatly. It is, after all, a drama and not real life.

But it is also responsible for solving a real-life crime. A crime that had been going on for many years right before my eyes.

Beth and I were sitting on our sofa one night. It was late. We'd just had one of those four-hour TV binges I mentioned in Chapter 8, catching up on Channel 4's ultra-stylish conspiracy thriller *Utopia*.

I had the remote control in my hand – there was no sewing to do – and I'd made a pretty good job of guiding us through the ads at speed all night, even if I do say so myself.

If we were sensible, we'd have been getting ready to go to bed. But I think the violence we'd just seen on screen had left us insensible. We were shell-shocked. My mind was numb but my thumb was nimble. With dead eyes, I was just flicking channels. I didn't know what I was looking for. I wasn't taking in what was on the screen. I was just moving up the channels – blip, blip, blip, blip – not giving anything a chance, just constantly moving it on.

And then something made me stop. It was an episode of *Waking the Dead* but I didn't know that immediately. I'd stopped because of a face. I'd seen a face I recognised. But it was out of context.

'Who's that?' I asked.

'Who's what?' asked Beth.

'That guy.' I paused the TV. 'Him.'

'I don't know.'

'What's he been in?'

'I don't know.'

'I hate not knowing.' I shrugged and hit play again. 'It's going to bug me.' And then I paused it again. 'I've got it!'

'Got what?'

'His name.'

'Really?'

'Yeah. That's the man from the Cillit Bang adverts. That's Barry Scott!'

'Really?' Beth looked unconvinced.

'Definitely!'

'Well ... I suppose it looks *a bit* like him,' she said. 'But I doubt it is. It'd be a bit weird, wouldn't it, casting a guy from the Cillit Bang ads as a paramedic in a TV show? I mean, he's a *thing*, isn't he?'

Oddly, I knew what she meant. And she had a point. The man in those adverts was a *thing*. He was a real-life version of *The Simpsons*' Troy McClure: a celebrity-endorsement-spokespersony sort of thing. You couldn't do that job unless you had some kind of celebrity credentials, could you? Isn't that why he introduces himself at the start of the ads? All that '*Hi, I'm Barry Scott*' stuff only makes sense if we're supposed to know who Barry Scott is.

'But it really looks like him,' I said, although I was starting to doubt myself now.

'What show is it anyway?' asked Beth.

Actually she yawned a sort of 'wha-oh-i-i-eh-ee-way', but I knew what she meant. If being able to understand one another's yawnspeak isn't the key to a happy marriage I don't know what is. I pressed the remote to reveal the answer.

'*Waking the Dead*.'

Beth stood, yawning as she did so. 'Eh-aye-ee-ee-uh-eh-aw-ah-nye.'

'Well, I've seen enough death for one night too,' I said, 'but I want to catch the credits. I want to see if that's Barry Scott.'

Beth shook her head. Then picked up a cushion and threw it at mine. 'Suit yourself.'

I didn't stay up to watch the rest of the show. I can take a cushion-to-the-head shaped hint. But I did press the record button before I turned the TV off and the first thing I did the next morning was spin through the show – at a slick 30x – until I got to the credits.

There was no Barry Scott listed. There was a male paramedic. But he'd been played by Neil Burgess.

Hmm. Maybe there were other paramedics in the episode? Maybe Barry Scott's part hadn't been big enough to get a credit? Or maybe I'd been mistaken and Neil Burgess just happens to look very much like Barry Scott.

Laptop. Google. 'Neil Burgess.' Search.

The first two links that showed up were about an academic of the same name – a professor from the Institute of Cognitive Neuroscience – but the third link was for a Wikipedia page.

Click.

Neil Burgess may refer to:
Neil Burgess (actor) (born 1966), British television actor Neil Burgess (comedian) (1846-1910), American vaudeville comedian.

Click.

Neil Burgess (born 6 June 1966) is an actor best known for his portrayal of the character Barry Scott on the British and Irish version of the television advertisements for the Reckitt Benckiser cleaning product Cillit Bang.

My jaw dropped. The scales fell from my eyes. (It's that powerful a descaler.) Barry Scott wasn't real! This was like Father Christmas all over again. How could Barry Scott not be real? What did this mean? I'd been lied to for all these years.

And that's how *Waking the Dead* helped me solve The Case of the Cillit Bang Fibs. Nearly ten years of lying!

Cillit Bang was launched in the UK in 2004. The dynamic, aggressive name seemed odd at the time. What did it mean? Was 'cillit' – a made up and entirely meaning-less word – supposed to sound scientific? Citric? Or did it start as Kill It Bang before they decided to soften it slightly by changing the kicking kuh to a curly cuh? Or did some idiot with a bad cold want to call it Cilla Black and things just got out of hand? We'll probably never know.

Before Cillit Bang came along, other household clean-ers tended to be packaged in white bottles. The labels would either use gentle pastel colours or the clinical greenish blue of a surgeon's gown. The message seemed to be, '*Don't worry, I won't hurt you. I am kind. I am pure. I am clean.*' Not Cillit Bang. Garish purple and orange were the order of the day. The message seemed to be, '*Get out of my way, I am dangerous. I might melt things! But I'll bloody well take the dirt out while I'm at it!*'

Their advertising has always been deliberately blunt

too. In the early ads 'Barry' would be seen in a kitchen or a bathroom, or in some ill-defined studio that could have been a lab but could possibly have been a shop that sells only Cillit Bang ... but more recent ads have seen him sitting in a fighter jet or a drag car painted in the distinctive Cillit Bang colours. I think their presence is meant to say something about power and speed. Either that or someone was looking at the ad's budget thinking, *'Shit ... we've got another two hundred grand to spend ... what can we buy?'* just as a fighter jet popped up on eBay.

But Barry's location was never as important as his demeanour. There has always been something self-consciously wooden about Barry. He doesn't speak with a relaxed, easy-going tone. He shouts. His hand gestures are a bit creaky. When he walks, he looks like he's think-ing about how to walk. To me, all of this seemed to reinforce the idea that Barry was an expert of some kind who was there to endorse the product.

It works by reverse logic, doesn't it? If you were hiring an actor to front an ad campaign, you'd get someone who could walk and talk at the same time. You wouldn't choose someone who walks like C-3PO with a recently fitted digital-suppository and who talks with all the nuance of Frankenstein's monster. Those are the tell-tale traits of the not-used-to-being-on-camera. And if they're hiring someone like that it stands to reason that he must be bringing something else to the table. Knowledge. Expertise. Celebrity.

Was I imagining it? Do the words *'Hi, I'm Barry Scott'* really carry that much information? I started watching the ads online. Hearing the line over and over trying to work out how it managed to convey so much about who he was supposed to be.

I think it's the presence of a surname. In one ad, he starts with the line, *'Hi, I'm Barry Scott and I'm here with Jill, who uses Cillit Bang Grime and Lime ...'*

That Jill doesn't get a surname but Barry does seems significant to me. It's code for *'This is just Jill. Don't worry about Jill. You've never heard of Jill. Her identity is unimportant. But I – I – am Barry Scott. You've probably heard of me.'*

We're clearly meant to think, *'Oh yeah ... that guy!'*

It's not exactly obvious that he's a character. It's not as if he's Mr Muscle or Mr Sheen. Which is why I'd spent the best part of ten years thinking he was an obscure celebrity who'd somehow slipped under my radar. Maybe he was a DIY expert from a regional programme I'd never seen? Maybe he was a former footballer from the minor leagues? Maybe he'd been well known in the 80s? It all seemed to fit the brand. It's what made the adverts make sense.

I'm pretty sure that's what we were supposed to think. But the knowledge that Barry Scott doesn't exist changes everything. Suddenly the ads start to ring a bit hollow. Neil Burgess wasn't a wooden, shouty paramedic on *Waking the Dead*! He isn't *really* wooden. He doesn't *really* shout. Suddenly, what I thought was genuine naivety is exposed as the carefully crafted artifice it obviously was.

If Barry Scott is a character, what are his characteristics? How does the actor Neil Burgess approach the role? What is Barry's motivation?

It's impossible to unravel. Neil Burgess is an actor who's been hired to appear in a series of adverts playing the role of a man who's been hired to appear in a series of adverts. Huh?

Of course, I know actors appear in adverts. I know that the motorist whose windscreen has just cracked is an actor. I know that the woman who's late for work and doesn't realise she's tucked her skirt into her knickers is an actor. I know. I know. But I know these things *because* everything about those ads – everything about the way in which those ads are viewed – tells me that. Nobody thinks Mrs Knicker-Skirt is being followed by a fly-on-the-wall documentary film crew. She's an imaginary consumer in an imagined scenario. But she doesn't look right down the lens and introduce herself. When Carol Vorderman appears in an ad for Bioglan Super Fish Oil* she looks you in the eye and tells you that she takes them every day to keep herself healthy. We understand that these words are intended to carry more weight coming as they do from the nation's favourite brainbox beauty. Isn't that the point of this type of advertising? Isn't the idea that the spokesperson's recommendation should

---

* http://gor.mn/VorderOil

mean more to us because they're not any old Joe Schmoe? But Barry Scott is Neil Burgess and it turns out that Neil Burgess *is* any old Joe Schmoe. If he wasn't, surely he'd be saying, '*Hi, I'm Neil Burgess.*'

Did they focus-group various names to see which sounded most trustworthy? Does Barry Scott sound like a man who knows about cleaning but Neil Burgess doesn't? Why would you make the opening line of your adverts a lie if you didn't have to?

Adverts have to comply with rules and regulations. That's why Rimmel have to include their ridiculous on-screen small print, admitting that less than half of the women they surveyed agree with a particular claim about a particular foundation. It's also why, when Barry Scott is seen dipping a grubby penny into a bowl of Cillit Bang and then immediately revealing that the half that had been submerged is now as shiny as the day it was minted, there's a caption to tell us that it was actually in the solution for fifteen seconds. When we see him pouring Cillit Bang Stain & Drain into a preposterously filthy toilet and then restoring it to perfect cleanliness with one flush, there's a caption to explain that it was really left for ten minutes before flushing. When the same product is poured into a blocked sink and we cut to see the transparent U-bend, magically unblocking as soon as the Cillit Bang arrives, a caption informs us that it actually took fifteen minutes.

Well, surely *all* their claims should be subject to the same scrutiny. Including the claim that their spokesman is called Barry Scott. I want captions. I demand small print! Every time he starts an ad saying, '*Hi, I'm Barry Scott* ...' I want some text on the screen saying, '*Not Barry Scott.*'

Bang! And the lies are gone!

CHAPTER 24

. . . .

THERE'S NO NEED TO INVENT A NEW WORD FOR SOMETHING JUST BECAUSE IT HAPPENED ON TWITTER

If two people are having a row, they're having a row. If they're doing it on *Twitter* it's still a row. It's a fight. It's an argument. What it isn't is a *twargument*. (And it's definitely not a *twar.)*

Words like this fetishise Twitter. They make the medium seem more important than the message. The medium isn't more important than the message. That's why nobody ever had a telephargument. If someone tweets:

Blimey @Made_Up_Name1 and @Made_Up_Name2 are having a right twargument!

I read it as:

Blimey @Made_Up_Name1 and @Made_Up_Name2 are having a right argument! LOOK AT ME. I'M ON TWITTER! THAT'S RIGHT: TWITTER! ON THE INTERNET! TWITTER! ME! OMG!

There's no need for it to have another word. It's an argument.

Tweet-up – meaning to meet up with people you know from Twitter – is even worse because it's not at all clear that it doesn't mean to tweet something up in the way that things are sometimes talked up.

Please stop referring to people on *Twitter* as *tweeple*. And especially not as *tweeps*. It's twee bollocks. (And *that* isn't a twitter phrase for small balls.)

I've seen *twarbage*, *twatch*, *twictim*, *twidiot*, *twidiculous*, *twignorant*, *twitchfork*, *twoyeur* and, Lord help us, *twroll* all used and each and every time they've made me wince. But the worst example has got to be *twife*. No, sir, she is not your *twife*. She's your bloody wife. You twincompoop.

CHAPTER 25

· · · · · · · · · · · ·

TWITTER ISN'T THE TWOLUTION FOR
TWALL OF LIFE'S TWOBLEMS

T witter. It occupies an extraordinary place in our lives right now. At least, that's true as I type this. By the time you read these words it might well have been nudged aside by some other social network. But I doubt it.

Twitter has become the de facto bellwether of public opinion. '*Twitter users expressed their outrage*,' screams one paper. '*People on Twitter rushed to show their support*,' crows another. A pipsqueak pop star can send a tweet with just fifteen words in it, and 24 hours later, three articles, each 1,000 words in length, have sprung up to dissect it. All of this makes Twitter feel important. And because it *feels* important, it *becomes* important. It is a self-fulfilling prophecy; a never-ending feedback loop. The more import we give it, the more important it becomes.

Now, I *like* Twitter. I use Twitter. It's just the veneration of it that makes me uncomfortable. (Come to think of it – venerating *anything* makes me uncomfortable.) I worry that the more people look to Twitter to solve their problems, the less likely they are to look elsewhere. It simply can't be the panacea some people seem to think it is.

I'll give you three examples of what I mean. It's tweets like this:

> **@Made_Up_Account**
> Please RT* to show your support for <??????????]

And:

> **@Made_Up_Account**
> Please RT. Let's get <??????????] trending**

And finally:

> **@Made_Up_Account**
> @DaveGorman Hi Dave. I'm doing a sponsored run/
> walk/bike-ride/sky-dive/silence/whatever to raise
> money for <??????????] please RT.

I can already feel you bristling at the third example. What kind of a monster would have a problem with that? Surely

---

* For those of you unfamiliar with Twitter, I should probably explain what 'RT' means. It's an abbreviation for 'retweet'. To retweet something is to repost – or forward on – a tweet originally sent by another user.
** Twitter has a list of 'trending topics' that is, one assumes, generated by an algorithm. It can be filtered in different ways – for example, geographically – but essentially, if a word is trending, it's being used in a lot of tweets.

only the world's most curmudgeonly scrooge could think of anything negative to say about a well-meaning tweet like this! Well ... let's go through them one by one and, hopefully, you'll see that I'm really not the charity-hating ogre you might currently suspect.

So ... first the *'Please RT to show your support for ...'* tweets. This might be for a tangible good cause, or a more abstract concept. I've been asked to retweet things to show I'm for firefighters and also to show that I'm against racism. And every time I resent the sense of judgement. If I don't comply I'm suddenly a racist who wants your house to burn down? Twitter seems to have created a world in which no thought exists unless it has been expressed. I like to assume that other people are pro-firefighter and anti-racist. I don't want to demand that everyone states it. I'd rather we demonstrated how against racism we were by, y'know, not-being-racist.

'I showed my support for the nurses, today.'

'I thought *everyone* supported nurses. Who *doesn't* support nurses?'

'Well, *maybe* you don't?'

'Of course I do!'

'Really? Did you *show* it today?'

'Well, no. Have I missed a news story? Are they on strike or something?'

'No, no. It's just someone decided we should all show our support for them today. No reason.'

'Really? Who started it?'

'I don't know. But they must be great. Just look at what they did for the nurses.'

'I don't get it. What did you do?'

'Me? I tweeted *my* support.'

'What?'

'Well, strictly speaking I retweeted something from someone else, but it was *very* clearly understood that it *was* a show of support.'

'Really? Did "*the nurses*" see it? Were they asking for it?'

'I don't know.'

'Was it for *all* nurses? Worldwide?'

'Mmm ... I guess so ...'

'Dental nurses?'

'Yeah.'

'What about nurses working in exploitative plastic surgery clinics?'

'Well ... probably not so much them ...'

'What if one of *them* saw it?'

'Well, they probably know I meant, y'know, *proper* nurses.'

'What about all the people you didn't tweet your support for?'

'What do you mean?'

'Well, did you tweet your support for, say, the oppressed minorities?'

'Um. No.'

'So you *don't* support them?'

'Of course I do ...'

'But how do *I know* that?'

What do such mass platitudes achieve? Is it just a way for a lot of people to make themselves feel better without leaving the couch? It's a salve for the wishy-washy conscience. Doing something is difficult. Saying something is easy. And saying something that everyone already agrees with is even easier. It just takes one click of a button to make the world weigh a little less heavily on your shoulders ... but the reality is that nothing has actually been done. I'm not pretending that my own life is an endless stream of active good-deeding – it's not – I just don't understand the idea that a tweet is, in and of itself, a thing of value.

Tweets like this foster the idea that Twitter is all it takes ... and that in turn feeds tweet-types two and three.

I can see what somebody's trying to achieve with a '*Let's get [whatever-it-is] trending*' tweet ... but then that's the problem. So can everyone else. It's transparent.

> **'*Carbon Neutral Golf* is trending!'**
> 'Ooh ... that sounds interesting ... what's it all about?'
> **'I don't know ... how do I find out?'**
> 'Just click on the words in the trending list and you'll see what people are saying about it.'
> **'OK ... here goes ... well, um ... well ... mainly people are saying *"Let's get Carbon Neutral Golf trending"*.'**
> 'Is there a link?'
> **'No. Just hundreds of tweets asking to be retweeted.'**

'Why?'

'So that they can get it trending.'

'So that …?'

'So that we'd see that a lot of people were tweeting about it.'

'And are they tweeting *about* it?'

'Well, not *really*. They're more just telling everyone to tweet about it.'

'So that …?'

'So that they can get it trending.'

The idea of the 'trending' list makes sense. Sort of. Well, it would if you were the only person who knew it existed. If someone from Twitter's research and development team approached me on the street and whispered, '*Hey Dave … we've got this secret feature that we like to look at in the office sometimes. Nobody knows it's there, but we can show you how to access it. You just click this link and you'll be able to see the ten most discussed topics on Twitter right now … and everything that's being tweeted about them too!*', I'd be fascinated. I'd click on it in an instant. But I would never tell a soul that it existed.

Because the moment people know it's there it's obvious that they will compete to be on it and that means you're no longer looking at the same version of Twitter. It's supposed to be a window on to the world of Twitter but pretty much the only thing you can see through that window is people trying to push themselves to the front to be seen. The only thing they're raising awareness of is the fact that they're trying to raise awareness of something and ultimately that just seems a little absurd. You might as well march down the street chanting *'What do we want?' 'To be on a march!' 'When do we want it?' 'Now!'* for all the good it does.

And yet you just know that every time something as inane as *Carbon Neutral Golf** trends, somewhere a brand manager is patting himself on the back and congratulating his team on a job well done. *'We educated no one … but we made it trend!'*

People want to trend because trending exists. It feels tangible. You can put it on your record of achievement. But as achievements go, isn't it only meaningful for something to trend because people are, y'know, *actually* talking about it?

I once saw someone ask Jim Carrey to help them get something trending, to help publicise the opening of a new shop in Bradford. He didn't retweet it. Of course he didn't. Why would he? What percentage of his ten million followers would it be relevant to? Why would a Hollywood movie star tweet something that would be of no relevance to either a) him or b) 99.95 per cent of those who would see it? Wouldn't it make more sense to publicise a shop in Bradford, by, I don't know … handing out some leaflets in, say, Bradford?

---

* Just to be clear, I made up the phrase 'Carbon Neutral Golf' and have no idea what it could or would be. But if it does exist, it's a coincidence.

Which leads me to the tricky area of the charity tweet. In part it's a tricky area because it opens up the idea of a them-and-us Twitter. All are equal on Twitter. Unless you're concerned with how many followers you have, in which case some people are more equal than others. Some people have a lot of followers and some people don't. And so the egalitarian view is that those who are blessed with a multitude are beholden to help those who are not. They must spread the love. They must help those doing good works reach a wider audience.

Of course the moment we think of Twitter as a world of haves and have-nots, we try to work out which team we're on. And some of you will have decided already that we are on different teams; that I am one of *them*. And that means your '*Well, he would say that … that's what they're like*' radar kicks in. But I'm not one of them. Because there is no them and us. There are no teams. Forget about numbers. They aren't important. Twitter really is just a swirling mass of people, doing their own thing, shaping it to their own ends. And they really are all equal.

There's a simple reason I have an issue with tweets like this:

@Made_Up_Account
@DaveGorman Hi Dave. I'm doing a sponsored run/ walk/bike-ride/sky-dive/silence/whatever to raise money for <??????????] please RT.

They don't work.

That's it. That's my *only* objection. I should probably tell you how I arrived at that conclusion because it certainly wasn't immediately obvious. The first time I received a tweet of this nature I retweeted it with alacrity. The person asking had a hundred or so followers. It only took a split second for me to dangle their fundraising page under the noses of thousands of people. I could see no reason not to do so. It made them happy. They thanked me. That made me happy. We were the good guys. It was a win–win.

But the next twenty tweets I received were all from other strangers who were also doing sponsored runs, walks, bike rides or sky-dives and they were all hoping I'd promote their endeavours too. In an hour I received in excess of 50 all but identical requests. I didn't know what to do.

Should I retweet them all? Surely not. That would be useless for *all* of them. I don't think tweeting 50 links to 50 charities is 50 times better than tweeting one. In fact it's probably 100 times worse. If you were walking into a train station and 50 different people approached you, each rattling a different collection tin for a different good cause, you'd be far more likely to skip past them than you would if there was just the one. Why would anyone continue to read my tweets after the tenth, twentieth or thirtieth identitweet?

So maybe I should pick and choose the most deserving of them and shine a light on three or four? How could I possibly do that? How could I begin to audit 50 charities? And what message would it send to the rejected? And if I did so – if I retweeted *just* three or four of them – what would happen then? If tweeting just one leads to 50 more requests, what will happen if I tweet four? Will it grow exponentially? An hour earlier, I'd been smugly patting myself on the back for my good deed and now I was feeling lost in the middle of a complex moral maze. I didn't know which way to turn.

'*Oh, woe is you!*' you're thinking. '*It was still good for that first charity, wasn't it? So what if you felt a little bit awkward as a result? It's not all about you, Dave, it's not all about you.*'

Well, no. Of course it's not. But my issue here is not just the awkwardness that accompanies that poor-me-stuck-in-the-middle feeling … there's more to it than that.

On an average day I receive between five and twenty such requests. For a while I fell into the habit of retweeting the odd one – something chosen on a whim – once or maybe twice a week. And every time I did, 50 more would arrive and I just got used to the pattern of it all and accepted it as part of the deal of life. Retweeting one felt like offering a seagull one of your chips. You know that doing so will mean you're suddenly surrounded by a flock of seagulls who all want chips and you know you can't oblige … but that first gull looks so hungry.

And I'm already feeling guilty for that analogy because I realise I've just described nice-people-doing-things-for-the-good-of-others – *the best kind of people* – as selfish seabirds and I know that's not right at all. But it does illustrate something about the moment before you click the button and retweet something.

I'd pause. Is this *really* the one I want to retweet? Am I *really* comfortable with this choice? Because in the next hour, 50 people – strangers, all of whom are honouring relatives and fighting good fights – are going to ask me to do the same and I know that I can't and that I will feel awful and so I really have to believe that *this* one is the *right* one. If you're not careful it's easy to feel paralysed by the projected guilt and shame.

Even so, it was a long time before I stopped to wonder quite how nourishing the chips actually were. Who is sponsoring Joe Bloggs' fun run just because I told them about it? Why didn't it occur to me to question that sooner? Ego, I imagine.

I wanted to test it somehow. I wanted to find out how effective they were. But the idea of retweeting something for charity as part of an experiment made me feel dirty, so instead I looked around for something I could simply observe. I searched Twitter, looking for the right kind of account. I found one. I'm not going to identify it because the specifics are not important and I don't want someone who clearly had the best of intentions to feel belittled or picked on. They were a very dedicated fundraiser.

For a week, I observed their Twitter activity and at the same time I kept a track of their fundraising page, trying to see if I could gauge the impact of one on the other.

Here's what I saw. Every day, at about nine in the morning, they would start tweeting. And they wouldn't stop for a couple of hours. Each tweet was identical but directed at a different 'high profile' twitter account. '*We're raising money for* [??????????] *Please RT*.'

They appeared to be working their way through a *Who's Who* of British micro-celebrities, cut and paste, cut and paste, cut and paste. They would tweet another two-hour session in the middle of the afternoon and a third in the evening. Sometimes they'd be targeting new people, but often they would be starting in the same place. A certain TV chef received their pleas three times a day, seven days running and didn't respond to any of them.

Which probably explains why, in between the constant flow of cut-and-paste tweets, there would be the occasional explosion of rage. '*Why is nobody RTing this?*' they'd tweet in desperation. '*Why can't they see how important this is? Why does nobody care?*'

I can see this from both sides of the fence. The person doing the asking simply can't comprehend why they are being ignored. They're not asking for much. All they want is for someone to make one mouseclick. They don't know that hundreds of other people are asking for the same and for causes that are every bit as good as theirs. They don't know that people are simply paralysed by it all. I very much doubt that the chef was sitting in his ivory tower, sharpening his knives and sneering at their tweets. I imagine he was sitting there thinking, '*Shit … how many of these can I do? How many is too many? How few is too few? Aagggh!'*

Then, one day, after four days of getting nothing, three different people retweeted them. All in one morning. One was a 'nation's sweetheart' TV presenter. One was a former pop-star. The other was an account connected to a breakfast show on a commercial radio station. The largest of the three had half a million followers.

That evening, the total on their fundraising page had gone up by – drum roll, please – just £15. They had received two donations that day. That's just two dona-tions that might – or might not – have come about *because* of those celebrity retweets. Fifteen quid is not to be sniffed at. It's definitely better than nothing. But put it in context. They were putting six hours a day into Twitter and had gone through four fallow days before this one. So the best-case scenario is that 30 hours of tweeting had raised an extra fifteen quid. I don't think 50 pence an hour is a great return. Wouldn't it have been better to put that energy into organising a bake sale? Or washing some cars? Or doing whatever the hell else people used to do before Twitter led them to believe there was a shortcut and that all you had to do was, say, ask a weatherman to tell his followers about it?

Because – and this is the horrible, unfortunate, uncom-fortable truth – strangers don't care. No. That's not right. They *do* care, but there are thousands of things for them to care about and your fun run just doesn't separate you from the herd. Nobody sponsors a stranger to do a bungee jump because bungee jumps are fun. They sponsor their dad, their cousin, their boyfriend's sister or Clive from accounts to do a bungee jump out of a combination of respect and social pressure. Knowing Clive from accounts means knowing how fearful he is of heights. It means being able to imagine his face as he takes that step into the unknown. And it means facing him in the queue at the works canteen five days a week and having to meet his eye. And you don't want to do that if you didn't sponsor him and you know full well that he sponsored you for that swim you did eight months ago.

You can pretend you're better than this all you like – and maybe some of you are – but I think, deep down, most of us know that we don't give a tenner to a stranger running a marathon just because Amanda Holden pointed out it was happening. Because most of us know someone who's running a marathon and we'd rather sponsor them.

You have to be doing something extraordinary – ten marathons in ten days, visiting both the South and North Poles, flying across the channel in a pedal-powered bike you built in your own shed – and for a particularly touching cause too, I might add, before someone who's never heard of you is going to dip into their pocket on your behalf. If what you're doing is one-of-those-things-that-people-do-for-charity and the cause you're raising money for is one-of-those-charities-that-people-do-these-sort-of-things-for then it's highly unlikely you'll get many strangers backing you because the voice they'll read your tweet in is the voice of Charlie Brown's teacher. As a rule of thumb, if you're not asking strangers to sponsor you face to face because you fear rejection, then it's even less likely that they'll do so if you ask them online.

I hate the idea that someone who's tweeted that kind of thing might be reading this and feeling bad. I know that it is only ever motivated by kindness. And I don't want anyone to read these words and think I'm describing an unkind and uncaring world. If anything, I think it's the opposite. We live in a very caring world. We live in a *very* giving world. Which is why there are so many people doing so many things for so many charities. So many that, I think, sponsoring the people you know feels like the only sane way of choosing between them.

Here are some numbers that do count. JustGiving.com is one of the main fundraising websites. It boasts that it has enabled 21 million people to raise £1.5 billion for over 13,000 charities since its launch in 2001. *That's* not a sign that people don't care for one another. But it is a clue to the sheer numbers of people who are seeking sponsorship at any one time. There is a huge value in so many people undertaking so many good deeds. Each person operates in a different social circle. Your local scout group raises money from theirs and my next-door neighbour raises money from his. But if everyone stops trying to do *that* because they've been seduced by the idea that Twitter is the magic bullet – the short cut that will take their fund-raising to the next level – well, then, I think they're likely to come up short. Because ultimately, it means everyone trying to piggy back on to the same crowd and that crowd can't see the good for the pleas. Twitter doesn't work for this, not because people don't care, but because they do.

I sincerely hope these words are taken in the spirit with which they're intended. I don't want to discourage anyone from fundraising for good causes and I certainly don't want to discourage anyone from donating. And I'm not for one minute suggesting that you shouldn't use Twitter to ask for sponsorship. The people who follow you on Twitter have chosen to do so. They are a part of your social circle. But the idea that people from outside of that circle will feel inclined to do the same seems to me to be fallacious.

I'm perfectly prepared to believe that I am wrong though. In fact, I encourage you to go ahead and prove me wrong. Before you go to bed tonight, why not go online. Go to Twitter.com and use the search function to look for the term '*JustGiving.com*'. You'll see a selection of tweets containing links to different fundraising pages. Pick one. Any one. Just at random. Donate something. Or don't. It's up to you.

CHAPTER 26

. . . .

WHY DOESN'T THE SUN TRUST ITS OWN PUNS?

There's something terribly disheartening about explaining a joke. Nobody ever comes out of it well. If you need a joke explaining to you, it's almost always too late for you to actually find it funny. At best you come away from the explanation thinking, '*Oh … I see … so that's why other people found it funny.*' Which is no substitute for a laugh.

Someone probably needs to explain this to the editorial team at the *Sun*. Its headline writers love a wisecrack or a pun. They've set the standard against which other tabloid headlines are judged. But they seem crippled by a fear that someone, somewhere won't get the joke … and so find themselves weakly explaining them with alarming regularity.

By way of an example, let me tell you about a 2011 story about George Michael being left by his partner, Kenny Goss. I have no idea if it was true, by the way, but it was given the headline: **'George solo as Kenny wakes**

up and go-goes.' That's the sort of thing that would probably elicit a chuckle from most *Sun* readers. It tells the story with a dash of humour. It is, in many ways, what tabloid headlines are meant to be.

But am I the only one who feels patronised by the article's third sentence? '*Worried friends of the former Wham! singer – whose hits include Wake Me Up Before You Go-Go – had been warning him he risked losing Kenny.*'

It might as well read: 'Worried friends of the singer – *we interrupt this sentence to explain that our headline was a joke. It's a reference to one of his songs. Get it? Please don't think we wrote "go-goes" for no reason! Now read the headline again and this time don't tut to yourself about our odd choice of words. I know you won't actually laugh. But at least give us some credit. We're not the idiots. In fact if you'd bothered to do your George Michael homework and familiarised yourself with his back catalogue, you'd have got that. Now who's stupid?* – had been warning him he risked losing Kenny.'

It just looks so defensive and embarrassed to be there.

Of course, when a story is about a famous musician the puns almost always relate to their body of work. So an article about Paul Weller falling over drunk gets the headline '**Paul's goin' on-the-ground**', an article about Mick Jagger appearing at an event with David Cameron gets the headline '**Sympathy for the Dave-il**' and an article about Madonna taking her kids to a school in Malawi is headlined '**Papa don't teach**' – and in each piece the same clunky format is used. Weller *has* to be referred to as 'the "Going Underground" singer', Jagger as 'the "Sympathy For The Devil" singer' and Madonna as 'the "Papa Don't Preach" singer' and each time I read it I think, '*Yes ... we know! And if you thought we didn't know, why the hell did you make it the headline?*'

Surely those who don't know simply don't care. Nobody is going back and laughing at the headline because the eighth sentence tipped them off, are they? (Well, they're definitely not with the 'Sympathy for the Dave-il' one.)

If you don't think this explanatory turn of phrase is odd, then I think you must read too many tabloid news-papers. You've got used to it. You've become immune to the nonsense. You think it's just-the-way-they-write-in-the-papers-innit? But try using this sort of turn of phrase yourself in conversation sometime and the oddness will instantly reveal itself.

Let's imagine that Paul McCartney was on TV last night and at work this morning one of your colleagues has asked you what you thought of his performance. Try saying, '*I thought Paul McCartney – whose post-Beatles hits included "Mull Of Kintyre" and "The Frog Chorus" – was great last night. Really good.*'

Just try it one time. You will be stared at.

If you work in an office, the next time it's your turn to make the tea, try saying something like, '*And would Sarah – who recently transferred from the Peterborough branch and is married to a teacher called Bob – like a cup of tea while I'm making one?*'

Sometimes things gets impossibly convoluted and the poor souls end up tying themselves in knots. In November 2012 the *Sun* ran a story about the then Manchester United manager, Alex Ferguson, meeting Daniel Craig's mother on a plane. The point of the story was that Fergie tells her there'll always be a ticket for her son at Old Trafford if he wants one despite the fact that Daniel Craig is a devoted fan of the side's most fervent rivals, Liverpool. There are a lot of ingredients there and I think you have to give them credit for a headline that manages to neatly combine both the James Bond and Manchester United elements: '**Never say Neville again!**'

Good work, the *Sun*, good work.

Or is it? Now they have twin worries. What if people don't know there was a Bond film called *Never Say Never Again*? And what if they don't know about the Manchester United player Gary Neville? What will *they* think of the headline?

Who cares what *they* think of it? Isn't the fact that they don't know *these* things something of a clue that *this* story probably isn't really their cup of tea? Isn't a story about a football manager meeting the mum of a James Bond actor most likely to be of interest to those who, y'know, know about football and James Bond?

Do the people at the *Sun really* imagine that large numbers of readers – odd people with no cultural reference points to hang on to – are scouring every page, devouring every word and demanding that sense be made of it all?

They must do, bless them, because the crowbars are out.

First there's, '*But Fergie – who has bent greats such as David Beckham and Gary Neville to his will – is not holding it against the actor and plans to see new film Skyfall.*' And then, '*The Red Devils' boss, who was en route to watch tennis ace Andy Murray in the US Open, also spent time with original 007 Sean Connery — star of Never Say Never Again.*'

Essentially, fifteen per cent of the article is a not-very-well-disguised Idiots Guide To Why The Headline Did Work *Actually*.

It's lazy to dismiss all *Sun* readers as idiots. But if the people who write it insist on explaining things on this level, doesn't it suggest that even they think their readers are numbskulls?

Chapter 27

- - - - - - - - - - - -

CAN TELEVISION PLEASE STOP ASKING PEOPLE, 'WHAT ARE YOU GOING TO SPEND IT ON?'

t's January. I'm watching TV. It's snooker. It's the final of the World Shoot-Out Tournament. The tournament is unlike most others in the sport. Snooker is normally a placid, slow, plodding affair. Finals might involve 35 frames of snooker played over two days. Not in the World Shoot-Out. The final – like all other matches in the tournament – lasts no more than ten minutes. It is a crash, bang, wallop form of snooker where every match is just one frame in length and players are penalised if they don't play quickly enough. The different format creates a different kind of atmosphere. It is not the reverential silence you normally associate with the green baize. It is more Christians vs Lions than that. The Blackpool crowd is boozed up and rowdy. The tournament is contested by the top 64 players in the world. On this occasion, Mark Allen and Martin Gould have won through to the final. As is often the way in this quick-fire format, it is a bit of a one-sided affair. Allen doesn't get much of a look in and Gould runs away with it, winning by 104 points to zero.

It's a big win for a player who's ranked just outside the top sixteen. He gets £32,000 for his efforts. The trophy is presented. The crowd cheers. And then there are the usual post-match interviews. No matter what the sport, these things always follow the same format. The winners feel great. The losers are gutted. It's not so much a conversation as a dance where everyone knows the moves.

It's easy to be scathing about the inarticulacy of footballers and their sick-as-a-parrot/over-the-moon clichés, but what else are they expected to say? If you want to hear them discuss the socio-economic repercussions of the game you'll need to ask them different questions. Post-match interviews aren't supposed to be probing. They're about emotion. But more than that, they are about the ritual. They exist to wrap things up for the viewers at home. It would feel odd if a game ended and the credits rolled without any further comment from anyone. So everyone dutifully goes through the motions.

'How do you feel?' 'Great.' 'Is this result going to give you confidence?' 'Yeah, I've always believed in myself and now I've just got to take that belief forward.' 'Have you enjoyed the atmosphere?' 'The fans have been great.' And so on, and so on, and so on.

And that's how it feels as I watch the presenter, Andy Goldstein, interviewing the victorious Martin Gould.

They exchange platitudes. They both seem to know the dance well.

But then Goldstein – a likable, self-effacing, self-aware sort – takes a surprising turn. Suddenly he says, '*So … £32,000 … what are you going to do with it?*'

This is the wrong dance. And if it doesn't strike you as an odd question you probably watch too much of the wrong kind of television. Surely it can only be over-exposure to daytime TV and schlocky big-money game shows that's to blame.

Television as a medium is patronisingly obsessed with what 'normal' people are going to do with money. Television wants to feel that *it* is changing people's lives. When a game show host says, '*So, if you won tonight, what would you spend it on?*', what they mean is, '*Go on … please tell us it's going to change your life. Tell us how important we are. Tell us that we have the power to change your life,*' and what they really mean by that is, '*Go on, tell us how normal you are!*'

I find it ugly enough in that situation, but at least I can see how it's come to pass. Producers know that viewers will care more about someone winning if they know that the money will be used to pay for a young couple's wedding, say. And they'll care more if they lose too. And so everyone goes along with it. Because everyone has accepted it is a part of the game show dance.

But it isn't – or shouldn't be – a part of the sportsman's after-match-interview dance. Whatever you might think about the rewards on offer to those at the top of their sport, the fact remains that it's *what they do for a living*. And asking someone what they're going to do with their wages is rude. And *that's* what Goldstein's done.

Perhaps the unusually rowdy atmosphere of the Shoot-Out has made it feel like a game show? Whatever the reason, he's just asked someone what they're going to do with the money they've earned by doing their job.

'*Well, mine is a high-risk profession where I don't earn money if I don't win games, Andy. And, of course, I'm self-employed and don't have a pension. So I'm going to put some aside for tax. I'm going to relax a bit knowing that my mort-gage is taken care of for a while, and then put some aside for the future because you never know when a lean spell is around the corner*', would probably be close to the truth. But, '*Mind your own bloody business, you nosey git! Why don't you tell everyone how much you're getting paid to present this and then tell us what you're going to spend* that *on?*' would be pretty fair, too.

Unfortunately, Gould just politely sidestepped the enquiry and said something non-committal about finding a way to spend it.

At the time, nobody in the arena seemed to find the question odd. I think it's because it has entered the realm of television cliché. We've become dead to its meaning. It's just become one-of-those-things-that-people-on-telly-ask. And having accepted it as such it has spread like a virus. So now, in the eyes of television, *everyone* is a game show contestant. No money can change hands without the question being asked.

On the daytime show *Cash in the Attic* the question is an integral part of the format. The show follows a simple pattern. A presenter and an antiques expert visit a viewer's home. They search high and low – but oddly, never in the attic – for objects of value. The antiques expert values them. Several items are taken to auction. Money is raised. So far, so good.

But not good enough. No, it is deemed important for the viewer to know what the money will be spent on. We don't want to think about a stranger just getting money! (Ugh. Ugly money!) No, we want to think about someone getting horse-riding lessons for their grandchildren! (Mmm. Lovely grandchildren.)

On the show's website, they describe each episode in a sentence. These are genuine examples: 'A couple hope to raise cash for a new sofa.' 'Thia Cooper hopes to raise money to take family and friends to a jazz club.' 'A couple try to raise enough money to build a new garden fence.' And, perhaps my favourite, 'Trevor Pearson tries to raise £1,200 at auction to modernise his cloakroom.'

It's gripping stuff.

Now I don't want to cast aspersions but whenever I've watched the show the participants have seemed pretty well-to-do. I've never watched it and thought, '*Crikey, if that vase doesn't make the top of its estimate, they'll* never *be able to afford that new patio furniture they're after!'* The sad reality is that the kind of people who have, say, £800 worth of antiques knocking about the house are normally the kind of people who wouldn't struggle to raise £800. That's just the way the world works.

So really the whole thing appears to be reverse engineered. It's not so much people going on the show because they need money for something as people wanting to appear on the show and then inventing something they 'need' money for. I'm pretty sure a fairer programme description would be, 'In this episode, a middle-class person thought it would be quite jolly to appear on television.' And there'd be nothing wrong with that.

Huge swathes of our television schedules have been devoted to antiques in recent years and the question 'What are you going to spend it on?' sloshes around those shows like cheap wine.

It is almost always inappropriate. If someone's selling a candlestick for 40 quid there is no point asking them what they're going to spend the money on. It's 40 quid. I'm not being blasé about it. I know that there are people in the world for whom £40 is a serious amount of money. But asking *them* what they're going to do with £40 isn't going to make for edifying viewing. *'Turn the heating on for once.'* *'Get some more expensive protein in my diet.'* *'I don't know, but at least it's saved me from going on the game.'* Those aren't the answers you want to hear on BBC1 at teatime.

But for most people – certainly most of the people taking part in these shows –£40 is a trivial sum. And so 'What are you going to spend it on?' is a deeply patronising question to which the honest answer would be, *'I'm going to delay my next visit to a cashpoint by as long as it takes me to spend £40.'*

And despite never having received an interesting answer to the question in the whole of their careers, they continue to ask it. Day in, day out they ask bewildered participants what they're going to do with small sums of money and day in, day out they receive the same answer: 'Oh … um … I don't know really … I'm sure I'll think of something.'

Why do they keep asking? What answer are they hoping to hear? What can *they* imagine spending £40 on that would be *so* entertaining to reveal? *'I'm going to change it into 50 pence pieces and have 80 games of pool.'* Is that it? How about, *'I have addiction issues, so it's probably going to go on 40 scratch cards. If I'm lucky they'll win £10 and I'll use that to buy another ten scratch cards'*? Is that what they want to hear? I'd like to see someone burst into tears and scream, *'I'm going to buy another candlestick,* actually!', but I know it's not going to happen.

The most interesting answer I've seen to one of these rude enquiries came during an episode of the BBC's *Flog It!*; a cosy show hosted by a twinkle-eyed flirt called Paul Martin. Christina is selling a German First World War helmet which one of the show's team of experts, Mark

Stacey, has valued at between £200 and £300. But the auction rapidly sails past those figures and by the time the hammer falls the helmet has actually sold for £820. Christina shakes her permed hair in shock. She appears to be a little overwhelmed.

'*I don't believe it!*' she says as she tries to catch her breath.

Our host is clearly genuinely surprised also and after a few words about how hard it is to value that sort of item he turns to Christina and asks *the* question. '*That's a lot of money!*' he says. '*What's the first thing that comes to your mind?*' He could leave the question there. But he knows the answer he wants. He doesn't want the mundanity of everyday life to encroach on his sunny little TV show. He wants frivolity. So he suggests an answer. '*Shopping?*'

Christina shakes her head. '*No,*' she says firmly.

'*No?*' Martin looks surprised. He's not used to someone knowing what they're going to spend the money on. He's finally found one! '*What?*' he asks, smiling in anticipation.

'*Um …*' Christina briefly, ever so briefly, glances to the skies. '*It's going to go towards a memorial for my father,*' she says.

Martin's smile evaporates as he instantly tries to recalibrate what his facial features should be doing. And it's in that split second – the moment in between the look of anticipation and the look of concern – that we see what looks like fear in his eyes.

It is a look that screams, '*Shit! Why didn't one of the researchers tell me about the dead dad? I wouldn't have glibly suggested shopping if I'd known about the dead dad!*'

Of course, it's easy to avoid getting an answer you don't want. Just stop asking the bloody question!

CHAPTER 28

• • • • • • • • • • • •

NOBODY CAN EXPLAIN HOW THEY KNOW
WHAT A TRUMPET IS. THEY JUST KNOW

While the question '*What are you going to spend it on?*' has travelled from studio game shows through the land of antiques-related daytime TV and ended up sounding like a reasonable question to ask a professional sportsman, the game show industry has been busily cultivating new ways to patronise members of the public that are all its own.

When I was a kid every TV game show seemed to be the same. Bob, Bruce, Jim, Jimmy or Des would ask the questions and nice middle-class couples would answer them. Along the way the host would look at his cards and say something like, '*So, Keith, I believe there's a funny story about how you and Janet met?*', and Keith would tell the story and Janet would blush.

There might be an element of luck involved in the game, but essentially it would be a general knowledge quiz in disguise and at the end of it the triumphant couple would win a small hatchback.

A car was the biggest prize imaginable back then although, if you were unlucky, you might find yourself competing for a caravan instead. That must have been especially galling if you didn't actually own a car. Imagine having to find another game show to go on, just to try and win something to tow your first prize home! (Of course, it could be worse; if you were on *Bullseye*, it was, famously, sometimes a speedboat.)

These prizes look modest by today's standards and there's a reason for that. Up until 1993 they simply weren't allowed to be more generous. The 1981 Broadcasting Act capped prizes at six grand. When you consider that, in 1988, the average price of a car was over £12,000, you can see that it wasn't even especially nice cars that were up for grabs.

Of course, the cars and caravans were only available on prime time shows. Smaller shows had smaller prizes. A daytime quiz might offer a couple of hundred quid. Or – more likely – a cut-glass tankard and a sense of pride.

But in 1993 the rules were changed and suddenly there was no upper limit. TV producers could give away *any-thing* they wanted. In 1995 the producers of Shane Richie's *Lucky Numbers* wanted to give away twenty grand – Britain had never seen anything like it. But it wasn't the biggest prize on TV for long as later that year Bob Holness turned up hosting *Raise the Roof*, a game show with a £100,000 house as its jackpot.

Of course, in 1998 everything was blown out of the water when *Who Wants to be a Millionaire* turned up in the schedules. (I imagine the format had actually been devised a decade earlier and they sat on it for a while in the knowledge that *Who Wants to be a Six-Thousandaire* just wouldn't catch on.)

But if anything really demonstrates the seismic shift that has occurred in this field, it is *Deal or No Deal*. It's on Channel 4 at 4pm and has a top prize of £250,000. A quarter of a million pounds! And it's on the box while most people are still at work! My, how times have changed.

It's even more remarkable given that it's essentially a game of chance. No knowledge or skill is required to 'win' at *Deal or No Deal*. As much as the show likes to pretend there are various tactics and strategies that might give you an edge, it really is just a game about opening boxes and riding your luck.

But what *Deal or No Deal* is really about is people. No game show has put its contestants' personalities more front and centre than this. As such it is emblematic of an even greater shift in the game show terrain.

Most old-school game shows used to find out nary a thing about the contestants. *The Generation Game* was a notable exception, I suppose, but on most of the game shows of my youth it felt like the contestants were completely interchangeable. It meant you had no one to root for. Does it matter if the middle-class couple from Gloucestershire win the three-door hatchback instead of the middle-class couple from Kent? When the only things you know about them are that one couple met through their shared love of country dancing and the other met when he accidentally picked her suitcase from the baggage carousel at Gatwick Airport, you don't really care either way. Because every which way is effectively the same way. The anodyne and anonymous way.

But in the modern game show, getting to know the contestants is key. And when you know a bit about them, you naturally care about whether they win or not. It makes sense. You're more likely to 'come back after the break' once you've made even a tiny emotional investment in the outcome.

Of course, *this* is one of the reasons game show hosts ask the contestants, '*What are you going to spend it on?*' If a show is giving away a life-changing sum of money, they want us to know exactly how an actual life will be actually changed by it. And in these circumstances, I know why they do it. It heightens our joy when they win and our sadness when they lose.

The trouble is, this focus on the contestants' personalities has become absolute. And just as it is pointless asking someone what they're going to spend 40 quid on, so it is pointless trying to eke some personality out of them when they're simply answering a general knowledge question.

Watch any of the mass-produced shows of daytime TV – the quizzes with a few grand to give away – and you'll be able to tell that the contestants have been told to '*talk us through the answers*'.

The host doesn't even have to ask them. They've been given instructions. '*Don't just give us the answer,*' an eager young researcher will have told them, '*run us through the options and explain your thinking. Don't worry. You won't look odd. It looks much better on TV if we get to see a bit of your personality.*'

But it's a lie. You will look odd.

If the quizmaster asks, '*A trumpet is what kind of instrument? Is it A: a string instrument? B: a percussion instrument? Or C: a brass instrument?*', there is only one answer that won't make you look odd.

'*Brass.*'

Explaining *why* you think that can only succeed in making you look simple.

'*Well, my son is in the school band and he plays the trumpet, so I can tell you that it's a brass instrument, Bob,*' is not a sensible answer. It's not a sensible answer because you don't know it *because* your son plays the trumpet. You know it because you're an adult and you know what a bloody trumpet is. You knew it before you had a child. You knew it when you were a child. You can't remember when you didn't know it and so you can't possibly explain how you came to know it. You just do. And so does everyone else.

'*Well, Bob ... I know percussion instruments are things you tend to hit or rattle or whatever and I'm pretty sure string instruments tend to have strings ... so by a process of elimination, I'm going to say, um, brass,'* is not a sensible answer. You haven't worked it out by a process of elimination. You've worked it out by a process of knowing the bloody answer.

CHAPTER 29

. . . .

YOU THINK THEY'D ASK SOMEONE WHO RECOGNISES MOVIE STARS TO DESIGN THE POSTERS FOR THE MOVIES THAT MOVIE STARS STAR IN

D o you ever get the feeling you're being followed? It happened to me yesterday. I spent most of the day on various forms of public transport, trundling my way around London for a series of meetings. If you're interested I travelled on one overground train, three buses and nine tubes. Just not in that order. But wherever I went in the city – from east to west and from south to north – whenever I looked up, the same face was staring at me. To make matters worse, it was the face of Bruce – or indeed, Walter – Willis. Sort of.

I say 'sort of' because it had all the elements of his face and yet somehow it didn't look quite right.

Imagine the victim of a terrible crime sitting down with a policeman and coming up with a photofit that perfectly describes their assailant.

'But *that's* Bruce Willis,' the officer says. 'We can't put that out on the wires, people will think we're accusing Bruce Willis of a crime.'

'Well, make the eyes, nose and mouth bigger,' says the victim. 'And move them to the left a little …'

'What? Off centre?'

'Yes. Now … down a bit. There. That'll do it.'

'I'm not sure anyone's face looks quite like that …'

'No. But it'll do.'

Well, that's what the face looked like. And it was everywhere I went, its too-low and too-far-to-the-left eyes always staring down impassively at me.

The face, as you've probably guessed by now, was on a film poster. The movie being advertised was *Red 2*. It seemed to be getting blanket advertising all across London. Either that or it was being sparsely publicised, and every single poster had been placed with my travel plans for that day in mind. Maybe someone *really* wanted me to see that film?

There was genuinely some doubt in my mind as to whether it was or wasn't Bruce Willis. If you weren't paying it that much attention – if you only saw it on the wall as you walked down a Tube station corridor – you'd just assume it was Bruce Willis. But when I started taking in the details, doubt started to creep in.

So my eyes wandered around the poster, looking for a name. And the poster seemed to back up my suspicions. Because there was a name directly above the face and it wasn't 'Bruce Willis'. No, according to the poster this lopsided Willis-alike was actually called Catherine Zeta-Jones.

Hang on. That's not right.

I think maybe an artist's impression of the poster will help to shed some light on matters. You know how bad my apple was ... so please bear with me here.

It's not very good, I know. But then you have to bear in mind that neither is the original. What is supposed to look like a group shot is, on closer inspection, clearly a composite of individual photos that have all been Photoshopped in peculiar ways. (The staff at Yahoo!'s showbiz news page would love it!)

It's not just the placement of Willis's features on the wrong part of his noggin. There are plenty of other weird details. Catherine Zeta-Jones's neck looks to have been stretched and narrowed. Her head perches oddly on top, like a golf ball on a tee.

Of course these – and all the other obvious distortions – might *not* be the result of lazy Photoshopping. This is Hollywood after all. Maybe they've all had drastic plastic surgery? (Are they offering face-enlargement yet? It's only a matter of time.)

I assume that whoever designed this just couldn't do feet and decided to leave them off. I'm glad. I can't do them either.

But all this is by-the-by. The fact that a multi-million-dollar movie will pay for a massive poster campaign but not bother to make the stars' faces look right is odd, for sure, but it's not the most annoying thing on earth. And it's not even the most annoying thing on the poster.

It's the placement of the names that drives me to distraction. Common sense dictates that if you're going to line your actors up in a photo, their names ought to correspond. Supermarkets put their tins of beans on the bit of shelf labelled 'baked beans' and the spaghetti hoops on the bit of shelf labelled 'spaghetti hoops'. Why should actors be treated any differently?

This is the madness of billing. The classic example given to explain how billing works in the movies is the 1974 disaster flick *The Towering Inferno*. Both Steve McQueen and Paul Newman wanted to get top billing and the solution was to make them 'staggered-but-equal'.

PAUL
NEWMAN
STEVE
MCQUEEN

McQueen is first if you scan the poster from left to right. But Newman is first if you read it from top to bottom. McQueen is mentioned first in the movie's trailers, but Newman's name is the first to be fully seen when the credits roll. Both egos have been sufficiently fluffed.

I understand that these games will be played. Is it the actors' egos, their agents' dick-swinging lust for power or some combination of the two that fuels it? And what purpose does it actually serve?

Nobody looking at the poster for *Red 2* would be in any doubt as to who is considered the film's star. It's clearly Bruce Willis. His image is larger than all the others. He's right in the middle, front and centre. The pictures have been arranged to look as if they're striding towards you and he's leading the pack. So do we really need to see that his name is first in the list too?

When a different name is floating above each face like this, it just looks like the production company have hired a graphic designer who simply doesn't know who anyone is. It looks like they've taken some wild – and hopelessly unlikely – guesses. They appear to think that Anthony Hopkins is called Bruce Willis and that Bruce Willis is called Catherine Zeta-Jones. They think Catherine Zeta-

Jones is actually being John Malkovich and that John Malkovich is called Byung-hun Lee. That chap on the end that I would have assumed was called Byung-hun Lee is, according to the poster, actually called Helen Mirren while the Helen Mirren-looking one is called Mary-Louise Parker which is odd because there's someone on the poster that looks just like Mary-Louise Parker but apparently that's Anthony Hopkins.

Is creating that moment of confusion helping to sell the film in some way? Is it helping to sell the actors? I can't imagine Bruce is actually made any happier by seeing his name in the top left corner. Does anyone outside of the movie industry actually consider that corner of the poster to be the best spot? It's not something you read like a book. It's a poster. You take it in its totality. If anything, your eyes are drawn to the centre first and then you look for other details. Putting his name there doesn't make him look like the star at all. The image is already telling us all we need to know about his billing. So wouldn't that be reinforced by putting his name right there, in the middle, above his enlarged face?

It would definitely help me out. As it goes I'm not overly familiar with Mary-Louise Parker and Byung-hun Lee. I'd find it much easier to read the poster if I could put a name to a face without having to solve a logic puzzle first. If you're one of those 'I can always remember a face, but I'm terrible with names' people, this must be your nightmare!

The truth is that, for me, a decision that is supposed to enhance the reputation of the movie's star just makes me think a little less of him. I'll explain.

Imagine that poster looked exactly as it does but with the names corrected so that each one corresponds with its owner's weirdly touched-up face.

ANTHONY **HOPKINS** CATHERINE **ZETA-JONES** HELEN **MIRREN** BRUCE **WILLIS** JOHN **MALKOVICH** MARY-LOUISE **PARKER** BYUNG HUN **LEE**

If I saw *that* on a station platform my thought process would be as follows: *Ah. I see Bruce Willis is starring in a new film. He's an actor I enjoy watching. But not so much when it's one of those all-action, gung-ho things he does. I wonder if it's one of those? Probably not. After all, it appears to have some unlikely old people in it. Helen Mirren, John Malkovich and, bloody hell, Anthony Hopkins! That's impressive. Chances are this is a film where the story is more important than the explosions. Good. I won't let Catherine Zeta-Jones put me off then. I wonder what Mary-Louise Parker and Byung-hun Lee are like …*

But with the poster as it stands, my thought process is rather different:

Ah, I see Bruce Willis is in a film. He's an actor I enjoy watching. But not so much when it's one of those all-action, gung-ho things he does. I wonder if it's one of those? Probably not. After all, it appears to have some unlikely old people in it. Helen Mirren and ... who's that in the hat ... that's not Byung-hun Lee ... oh, hang on ... that's John Malkovich and ... why have they done this ... bloody hell ... this must be so that Bruce Willis's name goes first! What a tosser!

CHAPTER 30

• • • • • • • • • • •

IT'S ALMOST AS IF THEY DON'T KNOW WHAT THE WORD 'MATCHING' MEANS. ALMOST

While the *Daily Express* might use almost identical headlines from time to time, MailOnline has a strange peccadillo for 'matching' headlines of a different kind.

Consider, for example, the headline, '**Casually cultured! Sharon Osbourne and Aimee Osbourne wear matching blue jeans to visit art gallery.**' (7/3/13)

MailOnline understands that it's not a newspaper. In print, headlines tend to be snappy and eye catching. Online, things are different. The headline isn't there to catch human eyes. It's all there to catch search engines.

It would be more natural to refer to '*Sharon and Aimee Osbourne*' or '*Sharon Osbourne and daughter Aimee*' than the oddly clunky, '*Sharon Osbourne and Aimee Osbourne*', but that would be less likely to capture clicks from people Googling 'Aimee Osbourne'. The clunky headline covers more bases.

But that's by the by. Because really, I just want to

discuss their use of the word 'matching'. '**Casually cultured! Sharon Osbourne and Aimee Osbourne wear *matching* blue jeans to visit art gallery.**'

Matching? What exactly is *that* bringing to the table? Blue jeans are everywhere. They are probably the most prevalent garments in the western world. That two people are both wearing blue jeans isn't really worthy of comment, is it? You might well think, '*Well, they can't just mean that they were both wearing blue jeans … they must have been particularly coordinated blue jeans. They must have been the same brand or the same cut or the exact same shade of blue or something?*' But you'd be wrong. I'm looking at the picture right now and it really is just two people wearing blue jeans.

Here's another example: '**Rosie in her robe: Transformers actress and boyfriend Jason Statham sport matching dressing gowns.**' (3/1/12)

This is a story about the model Rosie Huntington-Whiteley and the film star Jason Statham being spotted in *matching* dressing gowns. But is it really remarkable that their dressing gowns match? I suppose you might think that buying his and hers matching dressing gowns says something about a couple and if you do, you might think it worth mentioning. But that isn't what's happened here. The third sentence of the article says, '*The Victoria's Secret model is seen here on her hotel balcony in Miami wearing a white dressing gown, matching that of her boyfriend Jason Statham.*'

They're in a hotel! They're wearing the dressing gowns provided by a hotel! Of course they're matching! It would be interesting if they were wearing mismatched dressing gowns. That would imply that, despite what they do for a living, one of them wasn't used to staying in nice hotels where gowns are provided! Or that one of them was so fussy they'd packed their own gown. But no. MailOnline have decided that the *interesting* thing is that the gowns are matching!

'The transformation's complete! Jetsetting couple Elizabeth Hurley and Shane Warne display his and hers matching looks.' (28/9/11)

In what sense were Hurley and Warne's looks 'matching'? The article's own words should help us get to the bottom of it.

'And the pair looked every inch the jetsetting power couple in their sleek matching outfits and accessories.

'While Elizabeth, 46, wore her obligatory skinny black jeans, teamed with a peach coloured T-shirt and a fur gilet, former cricketer Shane also donned black jeans, teamed with a tight black T-shirt which highlighted his newly slim physique.

'The couple took their coordination to the next level as well, matching Shane's tan to Elizabeth's top, and both opting for dark sunglasses and matching smiles.'

Let's unpack this. She's wearing skinny black jeans. He's wearing black jeans. They're not skinny. In fact, from the accompanying photo, they're kind of grey ... but they are both wearing jeans. Dark jeans. His are a bit washed out and baggy. Hers are jet black and a skinny fit. But they are both wearing dark jeans.

She's wearing a T-shirt. So's he. His is black and has a round neck. Hers is peach. It has a V-neck with a little lace bow. In fact, come to think of it, I wouldn't really call it a T-shirt.

She's wearing a fur gilet. He isn't. His tan 'matches' her top. Only it doesn't. Not really. Her top, you'll remember, is peach coloured. His tan is, well, more like a tan. How many tans have you seen in peach? They are, I'll concede, both wearing sunglasses. His have metal frames in the aviator style. Hers have large plastic frames and are a little bit Jackie O. Oh. And they are both smiling.

So the extent to which their 'looks' were 'matching' basically comes down to two things: dark jeans and sunglasses. Now, I don't know about you, but on those days when I wear sunglasses I often notice that other people are wearing them too. It's something to do with it being sunny. So really what we have is a couple heading into an airport on a sunny day wearing dark jeans. Blimey!

'Double-take! Brooke Shields' playful daughters sport matching school uniform and red hair.' (13/6/12)

Does the person who wrote this understand what a school uniform is? The word 'uniform' is a clue. And while I'm not a geneticist, I have noticed that red hair often tends to run in a family. I have no idea what the father of Shields' children looks like, but if they were at all surprised when their first daughter turned out to be a redhead, I bet they weren't at all surprised when a second redhead followed three years later. In what sense are either of these 'matching' qualities remarkable? And if the answer is that they're not at all remarkable, why the hell is MailOnline remarking on it?

The list of these not-really-matching, 'matching' head-lines goes on and on.

'Like mother, like daughter: Alessandra Ambrosio and her mini-me Anja wear matching ensembles as they run errands.' (4/11/12)

Reality: Mum's wearing a pink vest under a green hoodie, daughter's wearing a long-sleeved pink tee.

'All you're missing is the red! Selma Blair and son Arthur go for matching blue and white outfits for Independence Day.' (6/6/12)

Reality: Mum is wearing a pale blue, striped cotton shirt, baby is wearing a dark blue and white gingham Babygro.

'Little monkeys! Sarah Jessica Parker and Matthew Broderick's twins sport matching designer rain boots on family day out.' (14/6/13)

Can you imagine! They didn't get different wellies for their three-year-old twins! The shame!

'It's Posh-er and hips! Made In Chelsea's Hugo Taylor and Natalie Joel sport matching outfits ... but hers is cut a lot lower.' (13/7/12)

Reality: Um ... they're both wearing sunglasses.

'Push in boots: Jessica Alba and daughter Honor take to the swings in matching footwear.' (25/3/11)

Reality: They're not matching. They're just not.

'They're rather Petra-fying! The Ecclestone sisters step out in Cannes wearing matching loud trousers for shopping trip.' (21/5/12)

Reality: Well, they're matching in as much as a pair of bright neon-pink trousers could be said to be matching a pair of muted grey, leopard-skin print trousers. Which is to say: *not at all*. But they are both wearing trousers so at least there's that.

'Mark Wright finds the perfect playmate! TOWIE star and Pamela Anderson hit the Playboy Club in matching blue suits.' (17/9/11)

Reality: Neither of them are wearing suits and only one of them is wearing blue. Seriously. I'm not making this up. Weirder still, they weren't actually together. They did attend the same function. But they didn't arrive together, spend time together or leave together. Or wear blue suits. This is beyond strange.

If you doubt me on any of this, by all means visit the website – dailymail.co.uk – and try a search on the term 'matching'. But I warn you, after ten or fifteen minutes of clicking around you'll start to feel a bit unhinged. Doubts creep in. Maybe it's you? Maybe you're the one who doesn't know what the word 'matching' means? Maybe you're the colour-blind one? Maybe you're the one who's odd for not looking at a photo and thinking, '*My*

God, you're right! They are *both wearing shoes! What are the chances?!'*

Because it's hard to see what other version of events can make any sense of the steady flow of these stories.

This, I think, is my favourite:

'Just like Mommy! Jennifer Garner and little Seraphina wear matching glasses.' (18/12/12)

It's my favourite because of quite how quickly it disintegrates. This is the opening sentence to the article: *'It was a case of mother, like daughter, for Jennifer Garner and little Seraphina Affleck on Sunday who made sure to partake in their daily ritual of picking up something to eat in Santa Monica, California but did so wearing almost matching reading glasses.'*

It makes for pretty hard reading, doesn't it? I assume they meant to say, *'like mother, like daughter'* and one of the likes went missing. But even allowing for that, the whole thing reads as if it has been fed through some kind of translation software having originally been written in French. There are missing words and incomplete clauses all over it. And surely 'reading glasses' are glasses one dons for the purpose of reading ... which these aren't. But ignore all that. Just enjoy how the 'matching' glasses of the headline have become 'almost matching' glasses in the very first sentence!

The article goes on: *'Looking like an adorable mini version of her famous mother, Serephina struggled to keep her purple-framed glasses on, pushing them up her tiny nose with her finger.'*

You might have noticed that they've changed the spelling of Seraphina there, swapping out an 'a' for an 'e'. I suppose that's one way of guaranteeing they get it right at least some of the time. But more importantly, let's focus on the phrase 'purple-framed glasses'. How many ways are there in which two pairs of glasses can be matching? I can only think of three: the colour, the shape and, at a push, the prescription. I think we can rule out the third of those so let's consider the other two. Do you think Jennifer Garner was wearing purple-framed glasses? She wasn't. She is not a child. She was wearing brown-framed glasses. So it must be the shape, right? Wrong. They are completely different shapes. Seraphina's glasses have oval frames while Jennifer's are square at the top and rounded at the bottom. I can feel another of my artist's impressions coming on.

'Matching Glasses.'

The only thing they have in common is that they are glasses.

There has to be a reason why MailOnline so regularly, wilfully and blatantly misuses the word 'matching'. And I have a theory. It makes things sound a bit more newsy. It makes things sound a bit more like a story.

If you're not convinced, consider what happens to some of these headlines if they are shorn of their matching-ness.

'**Casually cultured! Sharon Osbourne and Aimee Osbourne wear matching blue jeans to visit art gallery,**' for example, would be just, '**Sharon Osbourne and Aimee Osbourne visit art gallery,**' while '**They're rather Petra-fying! The Ecclestone sisters step out in Cannes wearing matching loud trousers for shopping trip,**' would become simply, '**The Ecclestone sisters step out in Cannes for shopping trip**'.

Effectively, they all become '**We took a photograph of a famous person doing a thing**'. And while there might be some people out there who think that Sharon Osbourne visiting an art gallery is interesting or that two rich sisters shopping is news, when you apply the same logic to the stories involving young children it starts to seem just a little bit creepy.

What is the story in '**Double-take! Brooke Shields' playful daughters sport matching school uniform and red hair**'? Take away the 'match' factor and it's just

'**Brooke Shields' playful daughters**'. In essence it's a story about a stranger photographing a nine-year-old girl and her six-year-old sister on the way to school.

Take the 'match' factor out of '**Little monkeys! Sarah Jessica Parker and Matthew Broderick's twins sport matching designer rain boots on family day out**' and you're left with '**Sarah Jessica Parker and Matthew Broderick's twins on family day out**'. Ugh. Those are three-year-old girls you're gawping at.

'**Just like Mommy! Jennifer Garner and little Seraphina wear matching glasses**' becomes simply '**Jennifer Garner and little Seraphina**'. That's it!

I don't think they really care that the words are turned into nonsense the minute anyone looks at the pictures. It's too late by then. They've snuck it past you.

I've never really understood quite how looking at these kind of pictures is supposed to be pleasurable or taking them noble? In what way is taking a picture of Jennifer Garner's three-year-old daughter a reasonable, dignified or valuable thing to do? Forget that her mother is famous and explain to me in what way is it not a creepy way to behave? I just don't get it.

But by using the 'matching glasses' headline the suggestion seems to be, '*Y'know what … we weren't planning on taking a photo of them … but when we saw how coordinated their eyewear was, we just couldn't resist!*'

And people click on the link. And they read the first sentence and they see that the glasses are only supposed to be 'almost matching'. And then they look at the photos and think, *'Hang on, they're not matching at all!'* But their mind is already wandering and they've already forgotten why they clicked on it in the first place. And they haven't noticed that, really, the story was, *'We hang out around women and their children and take photos of them! Go on, have a look at them. Look. Look at them. One of them has been in films. Look. Look at her. Do you want to look at a different woman? Go on then. Look to your right. There's a whole load of links to stories about women you might want to look at. Some of them are in bikinis. Go on. Look at them too. Don't worry, we'll always find a reason … we can all pretend that we're not just looking.'*

Weird.

CHAPTER 31

- - - - - - - - - - - -

WHAT IS THE 'NEXT CUSTOMER PLEASE' SIGN REALLY A SIGN OF, OTHER THAN OUR DESIRE TO NEVER SPEAK TO ONE ANOTHER?

We don't do a weekly shop in the Gorman household. We live in an urban environment and we don't own a car so it's easier to just do the grocery shopping on an as-and-when-we-need-stuff basis.

Over time the two of us have taken on different shopping roles. We've never had a conversation about it, we've just fallen into habits that dovetail neatly. Beth buys most of our fresh produce. She likes to plan menus and try different things. She'll see a new or unusual ingredient in a shop, decide that we're having it for dinner that night and then spend five minutes looking for online recipes on her phone to help steer her to some other, complementary purchases.

I, on the other hand, take care of the less adventurous stuff. I restock the staples. By which I mean rice, pasta and so on rather than small metal paper fasteners. I make sure we always have milk, bread and cheese. Tinned tomatoes, frozen peas, baked beans, coffees and teas: they're down to me. I ensure we don't run out of washing-up liquid and laundry detergent. I am proud to say that since the day we married we have never once run out of loo roll. That's my doing. No wife of mine will ever worry about wiping. I will provide.

It's not exactly a taxing task and I find my mind wanders easily. Which is why, on 2 March last year as I queued at a till with my basket of boring everyday items, I found myself inventing a brand new game. I can remember the date so clearly because it's my birthday. That's why in our house the game I invented is referred to by the frankly unhelpful title, 'the birthday game'.

I suppose you could call it a board game, it's just that the board is the checkout conveyor belt and the pieces are whatever groceries you've bought and – crucially – the 'Next Customer Please' baton.

It works like this: anyone who is adjacent to you in the queue is an opponent. You play against whoever is before *or* after you. If you have both you're locked in a three-player game. *But* they must not know that they are your opponents. They must not know that they are playing the game. Under no circumstances should you tell them that the game exists.

Apart from that, there is only one rule: the loser is the first person to place the 'Next Customer Please' baton on the conveyor belt.

That's it.

What are those signs for? Are they really there to separate our shopping? Or are they there to separate us? Because as far as I can tell, they only really achieve one thing: they reduce human interaction to the bare minimum. They certainly don't speed up the process of shopping. They just make sure that more of it happens in silence. Without those triangular prisms of joylessness, strangers might have to acknowledge one another. Conversations might break out.

Would it really be so disastrous to have *my* Hobnobs rubbing up against *your* chickpeas? How much dialogue would be required to negotiate that moment when *your* groceries end and *mine* begin? Surely a till worker and two adult shoppers can make that transition happen smoothly in just a couple of words? A little pleasantry here or there is all it would take.

But apparently most of us aren't prepared to risk it. We'd really rather not *have* to smile at a stranger. We'd really rather not say, '*Oh, actually, that one's mine,*' if we can help it. Why bother with any of that when a physical barrier can be silently put in place instead? Delineation. Separation. It's a grocery apartheid.

I want us to not use the barrier. I want us to speak. I want us to smile. But I am rare. Almost everyone else on earth feels the need to separate. They come in different varieties.

1: The Early Interceptor

You're approaching a till. There's one person waiting to be served already there. All of their groceries are already at the business end of things, meaning there is a clear yard and a half of empty conveyor belt for you to work with. You're not buying much. You haven't even got a trolley. Just a basket containing a pint of milk and a loaf of bread. You would have to be a provocateur extraordinaire to place your medium-sliced wholemeal within a foot of the washing powder that's bringing up the rear of their weekly shop and yet the moment they become aware of your intention to join their queue they reach for the guard. They give their groceries at least two and a half feet of breathing space. Lebensraum.

This is a form of madness, surely. Does the 'Next Customer Please' sign really need to be deployed in this situation? Who in their right mind would think someone had put their groceries on the conveyor belt and left such a yawning gap? Surely the long uninterrupted hum of the conveyor belt turning over would be a bit of a giveaway. Wouldn't it?

Bip. Bip. Bip. Bip. Bip. Hummmmmmmmmmmmmmm mmmmmmmmmmmmmmmmmmmmmmmmmmmmmmmm mmmmmmmmmm. Bip. Bip.

2: The Huff and Puff Tut-Tutter

When an Early Interceptor finds themself *behind* you at the till they become instead a Huff and Puff Tut-Tutter. You're already at the till. They're approaching. Every fibre of their being knows that if the roles were reversed the sign would already be in play. They can see the vast expanse of virgin conveyor belt and it makes them anxious. They are desperate for you to set the boundaries. They loiter a moment. They don't want to assume. Maybe you need the *whole* conveyor for some large item that's yet to be revealed. Maybe there's an ironing board in your trolley and they just haven't noticed it yet. I mean, the shop doesn't even sell ironing boards but they're prepared to give you the benefit of the doubt. Or maybe you haven't noticed their presence. They want *you* to put the sign in position. They don't want to take control of the situation. But they're unable to take the teabags out of their basket until the sign is in place to tell them exactly how much conveyor belt they are allowed to occupy. You don't do anything. You can see there is no need for this artificial line to be drawn. But they can't cope. And so they cave in. With a heavy sigh, a huff, a puff and a tut, they reach across you and grab the sign. They place it very deliberately. It's not enough for them that the sign is now in play. They must know that you witnessed its arrival.

They are teaching you till etiquette. (Frozen peas and queues?) Their silent glower communicates a sarcastic, '*was-this-really-too-hard for you?*' Then – and only then – can they commence with the transfer of goods from basket to conveyor belt.

3: The Late Snapper

Late Snappers can be before or after you in the queue. They are the ones who fool you into thinking it's going to be a nil-nil draw. They don't appear to be bothered. Their shopping is on the belt. Yours joins it. Or vice versa. For a moment or two they think they're OK with it. I mean, the sign is nearer you than it is to them and they can see that you're not inclined to use it and so they think, '*OK, I can handle this. This guy obviously does things differently to me. But I can see the gap. The gap is obvious, isn't it? Anyone can see the line where one set of groceries ends and the next begins. There's no room for any confusion there. You know what ... I'm cool with this. I'm feeling kind of relaxed about it. It's like being in a taxi in a foreign country and there isn't a seat belt and you don't say anything because you don't want to offend anyone. It feels wrong. But it's a bit daring. And the chances are that no harm will come to any of us. This is going OK.*'

But then the conveyor belt jerks a little and a packet of biscuits rolls half an inch and even though the likelihood that we might end up having to talk to one another seems slight, the moment when we'll know for sure is rapidly approaching and they just can't stand it any longer. They give in. They go for the sign.

The chances are that you are one of these types. You are either an Early Interceptor, a Huff and Puff Tut-Tutter or a Late Snapper. It seems likely that you must be one of them because it is many moons since I've drawn a game. Everyone I ever encounter at a supermarket till wants the 'Next Customer Please' sign to insulate them from any unnecessary human contact.

After a while, I found winning every game became boring. I decided I wanted to earn a draw. I would only be happy if I could find a way of persuading people not to reach for the sign.

There is obviously nothing that can be done for the Early Interceptors, but I had hope for the others. But most of my efforts have failed. I have tried all sorts of things. I have tried instigating a conversation *before* the sign is used. I find people are a tad suspicious but surprisingly happy to chat. But if anything it seems to make them even keener on the sign. It's as if they're thinking, '*OK … I'll go along with this social intercourse but I'll definitely take precautions.*'

I've tried increasing the gap between my shopping and theirs. As the conveyor belt moves their groceries forwards, I shuffle mine back as if to say, '*Don't worry … I'm keeping these things apart my way.*' It doesn't work.

And then, finally, I stumbled across something that does work. I have found my way of taming people's instinct. It involves adding just one item to my groceries: a large bar of chocolate. It's simply the shape. People know it's not the right triangular prism. But it's enough. Placed with purpose, a large Toblerone does the job.

POSTSCRIPT

There's a fair chance that some of you have just been struck by a sudden desire for some Swiss chocolate. I'm sorry about that. It wasn't meant to be an advert but I guess it will function like one all the same. That's all it takes, isn't it: one word, one picture. That's enough to set the synapses racing. You weren't thinking about chocolate. You saw an image of some chocolate. All of a sudden you're thinking of chocolate. And so now you fancy some chocolate. That's how advertising works, right?

Well ... not always, no ...

CHAPTER 32

. . . .

I THOUGHT THE POINT OF ADVERTISING WAS TO TRY AND PERSUADE PEOPLE TO BUY YOUR PRODUCT

have a way of working out if someone likes football or not. Of course, I know you can just ask someone if they like football but I wouldn't call that 'working out'. Hercule Poirot doesn't *work out* who the murderer is by just asking everyone present if they slipped some hemlock into the colonel's tea and you don't *work out* the answers to a crossword by waiting for tomorrow's paper and looking up the solutions. No, I mean that I have a way of *working it out* without asking any direct, football-related questions. I don't need to ask someone who they support, or who their favourite player is or what their favourite goal of the season has been or anything like that. I just have to mention two words: *Rainham Steel*.

If their eyes flicker with recognition then I know that they like football. Or at least I can be fairly certain. I admit there is room for error here. I suppose there are other reasons they might recognise it. I guess you'd react

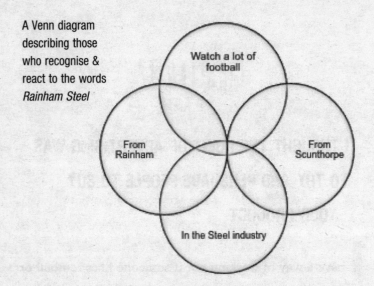

A Venn diagram describing those who recognise & react to the words *Rainham Steel*

Watch a lot of football

From Rainham

From Scunthorpe

In the Steel industry

if you were from Rainham in Essex, where the company is based. Or if you were from Scunthorpe, where they have a large distribution depot. And of course, it's always possible that you're a steel magnate in which case you'd be aware of them as a competitor or ally of some kind.

In practical terms, though, I've found my method to be foolproof. I guess I don't hang out with many steel magnates.* Broadly speaking, while the non-football fan thinks Rainham Steel might be a fictional detective ('*The name's Steel, Rainham Steel*') football fans invariably recognise it immediately as that-company-that-seems-to-advertise-at-every-football-ground-ever.

---

* It's impossible to say the words 'steel magnate' in conversation without worrying that the person you're talking to thinks you just said 'steel magnet' and is now thinking you're a little simple. cf. 'Badminton Horse Trials.'

It doesn't seem to matter what level of football you're watching. It might be the Championship, the Premier League or an England International at Wembley ... somewhere around the ground there will be an advert bearing the words Rainham Steel.

And that's all the advert will say. There won't be a logo. Or a slogan. It will just be the two words. Blue text. White background. Block capitals. RAINHAM STEEL.

I'm struggling to work out who these ads are aimed at. I've never sat watching the footy and thought, '*Ooh, that's handy ... I need some steel!*'

Everything else I see advertised on the hoardings makes sense to me. You get hoardings from mass-market brands and then occasionally – especially in the lower leagues – there'll be one from the local taxi firm or an independent butcher. And as you see them, you understand precisely why they're there and who they're aimed at. Of course a gambling website like *Bet365* wants to advertise to millions of viewers. Of course a clothing brand and a car manufacturer want to put themselves on display. We like to think we are dispassionate when it comes to brands, but we're not, we're really not.

I have not inherited my father's tigerish passion for cars. I haven't owned a car for many years. I have no interest in them. Motorsports leave me cold. I don't read about cars. I don't watch TV shows about cars. I can't remember ever having had a conversation with any of my friends about cars. And yet I am aware that I think that

Fords are probably quite reliable and that Volkswagens are going to hold their value better than most. I think Volvos are safe but pricey. I think BMWs are luxurious and I think Audis are quite like BMWs but less show-offy. I have a firmly held opinion that Fiats are light-weight and that Renaults are fun. And of course Skodas are much-better-than-they-used-to-be-*actually*-and-y'know-they-really-make-a-lot-of-sense-if-you've-got-kids.

If you're a petrol-head you might well be scoffing at my naivety here. Maybe I'm completely out of touch with popular automotive opinion. But it doesn't really matter if I'm right or wrong. That I have any opinions about these marques at all speaks volumes about the power of brand perception. My opinions aren't based on experience. I have no facts to back them up – I don't know that I've ever so much as sat in a Renault, let alone driven one. I can't identify where my auto-prejudices come from. Do they float through the ether? Have I absorbed them by osmosis? How big a part have adverts played? I can't recall a single slogan from a single car ad but they must have gnawed away at my brain subliminally or surely I'd have no opinions to offer at all.

And when you realise how powerful and pervasive our perceptions of brands are, it makes perfect sense for them to be advertising wherever they think our eyeballs will be.

But how many people buy industrial steel? When did you last buy some steel bearing piles? How many parallel flange channels did you pick up when you last popped to the shops?

Surely the influences that come into play when you're buying a car or a box of cereal, or a pair of jeans, don't affect the purchasing of industrial steel. A successful brand can give a mass-market product that indefinable, I-know-these-two-things-are-in-every-measurable-way-the-same-but-for-some-reason-I-just-prefer-this-one quality. That can't be a factor with steel, can it? Isn't one steel girder much like any other? I mean, if your universal beam is made of a material that meets the European Standard (EN 10025) and the dimensions meet the British Standard (BS4-1) then in what way is one going to be better than another? Isn't the point of setting these standards to guarantee that things are, y'know, *standard*?

If your company put you in charge of a £3 million building project, wouldn't you want to buy your steel components from whichever firm was best able to deliver them on time and at the right price? Wouldn't you shop around a bit first? It's not exactly an impulse buy, is it?

'*Well, I wasn't sure where to get any steel from … and then last night, I was watching the football and there it was! My friend Barry said he knew someone who could do it cheaper, but I said, "Y'know what, Barry, I like Rainham, I don't know why, I just do."*'

Y'know what? The fact that they've been advertising at football for as long as I can remember has made my mind up. Just to spite them, the next time I fancy buying some industrial steel I'm going to look elsewhere. That'll learn 'em.

Now ... what's going on on Twitter?

CHAPTER 33

* * * * * * * * * * * *

KIDS WILL BE KIDS WILL BE SPAMMERS

@TheFunnyWhale
@DaveGorman u guys gotta book @TheNickyParis.
19 yr old comic in NYC who is BLOWING UP he's
done a bunch of radio interviews check his page.

t's not the oddest thing I've ever been sent on Twitter. I was, at the time, hosting a weekly radio show but this seemed like an odd way to go about persuading me to have someone on as a guest. My first thought wasn't to check *his* page as instructed. No, my first thought was to check out @TheFunnyWhale's page.

There, the profile said that they existed to 'promote the funniest accounts on Twitter'. Fair enough. I wondered who else they were promoting. Surely there'd be tweets about a handful of different names, at least. There weren't. Almost every tweet was identical. Tweet after tweet for page after page this account had sent out the same message to hundreds of people.

@TheFunnyWhale

@[*a different username every time*] FOLLOW 1
OF THE BEST Comedians on twitter my pal
@TheNickyParis u'll LOVE his tweets! ILL FOLLOW
U! Tweets are perfect 4 RT

The only variation being tweets like the one I'd received encouraging folks to book him for their radio show, comedy club or whatever.

It was pretty obvious that Nicky Paris was @TheFunnyWhale and that @TheFunnyWhale was Nicky Paris.

As annoying as this kind of spam is, at I don't think this is something to be too scathing about. I can certainly see how tempting it must be. At the radio station I'd sometimes receive promotional CDs. They'd normally arrive with a press release explaining why this particular song deserved my attention and some airtime. They often contained boasts about how many fans were following the band on Myspace, how many plays they'd had on YouTube and how many followers they had on Twitter. But I knew that these numbers were now effectively meaningless. *Because* they had become the currency du jour, so people had worked out how to fake them. There are websites where you can buy 1,000 YouTube views for a dollar. Fifty dollars is enough to make your song look like it's 'going viral'.

The pressure to get involved in such shenanigans must be immense. Like the athlete who convinces himself that he ought to take steroids because everyone else is doing it, so a band – or their management – will feel tempted to spend some money buying fake popularity in the hope that they can then parlay it into the real thing.

I'd never heard of anything like that happening in comedy before but maybe the scene was different in New York? Maybe the number of followers a comedian had was deemed important there? The minute a club says to a young act, 'We won't book you until you've got 50,000 followers,' is the minute that someone starts trying to make it happen by any means necessary.

And because the world is so obsessed with these numbers – it sometimes seems as though *everyone* is desperate to have more followers – the only thing you have to offer people to persuade them to follow you is … a follower in return. But of course *you* can't offer to follow *them* back. *You* won't look popular if *you're* following 50,000 people. That won't look cool at all! So you offer people a deal. In this instance: if they follow @TheNickyParis then @TheFunnyWhale will follow them. Your numbers improve. Their numbers improve. Neither of you has to pay the slightest bit of attention to one another – that's not what it's about – just look at the numbers. Never mind the quality, feel the width.

It's in the nature of teenagers to look for shortcuts. Teenagers are in a hurry. They want success and they want it now. If society sends young people the message that success can be measured in social media presence, then what do you bloody expect? Of course some of them are going to manipulate it, if they can see how to go about it. All Nicky Paris was doing was using the tools available to him. Albeit in a clumsy, gauche and transparent way. I'd like to think the nineteen-year-old me wouldn't have been so venal. But maybe I would have been. I'll never know for sure.

Of course if you're going to play that game I figure you have to accept that, from time to time, you'll get caught with your fingers in the cookie jar. So – and yes, I know it wasn't big or clever of me – I sent @TheFunnyWhale a teasing tweet, just to let Nicky know that I was on to his ruse.

@DaveGorman
@TheFunnyWhale Wow! Have you ever tweeted anything else? It's as if your account exists solely to spam for @TheNickyParis.

And @TheFunnyWhale took it in good humour.

@TheFunnyWhale
@DaveGorman Oops! I guess it is obvious. Sorry. I'm just trying to catch a break. I'll take that as a no, then shall I? Nicky.

And then we both went on with our lives.

Oh. No. Sorry. I got that wrong. That wasn't how @TheFunnyWhale replied at all. Instead he threw a bit of a tantrum, told me I was being very rude and then blocked me.

Fair enough. I *was* teasing him after all. And it's probably a bit embarrassing to get caught out. But I don't think I'd describe my behaviour as 'very rude'. You can't really send spam and then get upset with someone when they reply saying, 'Oi, stop sending me spam!'

And his reaction just made me more curious. And I wasn't the only one. Several people got in touch to tell me they'd also received spammy tweets promoting Nicky Paris. But they hadn't all come from @TheFunnyWhale. One person told me they'd received the same from @TheFunnyLips while another told me they'd received it from @TheFunnyDiamond. A journalist who writes about and reviews comedy got in touch to say, *'There's loads of "TheFunny…" accounts. It'll be TheFunnyLion or Giraffe tomorrow. Always the same message about Nicky Paris.'* (He'd never looked up 'Nicky Paris' to see if he was legit or not because the tweets seemed so spammy to him that he'd just assumed every link contained within was toxic in some way and not to be trusted.)

When I'd replied to @TheFunnyWhale it had been like tugging at a loose thread. I did it thinking it would snap off … but, instead, a much larger fabric had unravelled in an instant.

It turned out that as well as being @TheFunnyWhale, Nicky Paris was tweeting as @TheFunnyHeart, @TheFunnyTooth, @TheFunnyMustach, @TheFunnyLips,

@TheFunnyBaby, @TheFunnyCake, @TheFunnyCupcake, @TheFunnyCherry, @TheFunnyPeanut and @TheFunny Coconut.

Oh … and also @TheFunnyDragon, @TheFunnyWitch, @TheFunnyGenie, @TheFunnyCroc, @TheFunny Cheetah, @TheFunnyCow, @TheFunnyKitty, @TheFunnyShrimp, @TheFunnyCamera, @TheFunny Diamond and @TheFunnyHouse.

Not to mention @TheFunnyDuck1, @TheFunnyFrog1, and @TheFunnyMouse1.

And that's just the accounts that were still active.* Some of his other accounts had been suspended. @TheFunnyOwl, @TheFunnyPanda, @TheFunnyGranny, @The FunnyBear1 and @TheFunnyBird1 amongst them. As well as the not quite so 'TheFunny'-titled, @BritBrit123123, @TheJokerWild1 and @JoyceJoyJoy1.

At this point it stops looking quite so innocent. It's no longer a teenager, naively trying to drum up a bit of support (or even just the appearance of support) with a few tweets from an ill-disguised alter ego. This is spamming on an industrial scale. And if eight of your accounts have been suspended … well, surely that's eight warning shots across the bow. It's hard to argue that you didn't know it was wrong when the powers-that-be at Twitter have nuked you eight times.

I wanted to know quite how industrial it all was so I

---

* I don't believe any of the accounts are currently active.

started adding up how many tweets each account had sent.

As you can see, it makes for a staggering 182,276 tweets from just 23 accounts. And this doesn't include the tweets sent by @TheFunny Whale or @TheFunnyGenie – both accounts he deleted before I could add them in – or from the eight different accounts that Twitter had suspended.

Assuming each of those accounts had hit similar levels – he was averaging 7,925 tweets with each identity – then that would take the total to 261,526. More than a quarter of a million!

And remember, these are just the accounts that had either been brought to my attention by other disgruntled Twitter users or that I'd found with the briefest of searches. There's no reason

Account	Number of tweets
TheFunnyMouse1	14,925
TheFunnyShrimp	13,125
TheFunnyCroc	12,670
TheFunnyPeanut	12,644
TheFunnyCheetah	12,102
TheFunnyHouse	11,697
TheFunnyCherry	11,547
TheFunnyCake	11,361
TheFunnyTooth	11,321
TheFunnyDragon	10,643
TheFunnyKitty	10,255
TheFunnyBaby	9,740
TheFunnyCupcake	9,494
TheFunnyCow	8,554
TheFunnyCamera	5,266
TheFunnyWitch	4,430
TheFunnyLips	4,421
TheFunnyMustach	1,798
TheFunnyDiamond	1,523
TheFunnyCoconut	1,270
TheFunnyFrog1	1,245
TheFunnyHeart	1,229
TheFunnyDuck1	1,016
Total:	182,276

to think I'd found them all. It certainly seems likely there were more. It doesn't seem all that fanciful to suggest that he'd probably tweeted more than 300,000 times.

And almost all of them saying the same thing:

@TheFunnyWhale

@[*a different username every time*] FOLLOW 1 OF THE BEST Comedians on twitter my pal @TheNickyParis u'll LOVE his tweets! ILL FOLLOW U! Tweets are perfect 4 RT

Nicky justified his behaviour by arguing that he got a lot of retweets. This was evidence that people liked what he was tweeting, that they liked what they'd found. So why should it matter that they'd discovered him through a campaign of this nature?

Well, he's certainly right that there's an audience for what he does. His comedy is about unleashing that outrageous, judgemental gossip that lurks inside us. He's a camp, bitchy character who tweets cattily about the likes of Miley Cyrus,* Britney Spears,** Kim Kardashian*** and Amanda Bynes.**** Every star – especially every female star – is deemed too fat, too thin, too drunk, too slutty, too square, too boring, too outrageous, too *something* and yet

* Pop star.
** Pop star.
*** Her again!
**** No idea.

he worships and adores them too. Because they're divas and so is he. His is a comically shallow world view in which having fabulous eyebrows and slim hips is all a guy (or gal) should aim for.

I guess he's pitching himself as a young, male version of Joan Rivers and there's nothing inherently wrong with that. Of course his tongue isn't as sharp as hers or his focus as pure but then whose is? It's something to aim for.

But does the fact that he gets retweeted really justify the spam tweets? I suppose it does in the same way that getting an order for a fake Rolex might justify sending that spam email. Personally, I'm not convinced that just because it works, it's OK. Especially when the people you're pissing off *can't* block you because you're regenerating with a new spamdentity as often as you please. If anything the fact that there is *some* substance to him just makes the spam even more annoying. If the energy required to send a quarter of a million tweets had been used more productively, just imagine what he could have achieved!

But it turns out you don't need to consider the argument anyway. It doesn't really matter whether you see a retweet as a validation of his methods or not. Because some of the retweets weren't all they were cracked up to be. Another Nicky Paris nom-de-tweet was soon unearthed: @Princess_Peach7. This Princess had sent 11,324 tweets and almost all of them looked like this:

@Princess_Peach7

@[*a different username every time*] YOU SHOULD
PROMO WITH @THENICKYPARIS! 5 RTs FOR
5RTs! EMAIL HIM AT [*email redacted*] TO SET UP
PROMO!!!!!

Which rather suggests that at least some of those retweets weren't posted because someone loved the content but because they'd entered into a mutually beneficial, you-scratch-my-back-and-I'll-scratch-yours social media Ponzi scheme.

And the argument falls down completely when you see some of the other tactics that were being used a few months later. I'll show you what I mean with three example tweets. I don't think Nicky was running any of the accounts that sent them. Nor do I know what, if anything, he was doing in return. But they are, I think, quite outrageously cynical.

I'm aware that some older readers might struggle to decode their meaning so I'll offer translations as we go.

Tweet 1 (Sent 30 April 2012)*

@TeamOf1DJB

#RT if you were born in 1992,1993,1994,1995,1996,
1997,1998 or 1999 so I can give you 500+new
followers. (must be following @TheNickyParis)

* http://gor.mn/1DJBspam

Translation:

This account is devoted to the pop superstars of the moment, One Direction and Justin Bieber.
If you are between the ages of 13 and 20 then I will make you look much more popular by somehow arranging for you to have 500 new followers. But for some inexplicable reason, I will only bestow this upon you if you are following Nicky Paris. Begin.

Tweet 2 (Sent 14 April 2012)*

@CuddleMe
RT if u want me to get jb to DM u RIGHT NOW.He's online ladies.I can text him for all u beautiful girls. Must be following @TheNickyParis,,

Translation:

You probably think my account is called Cuddle Me. But that's not actually an L between the D and the E, it's a capital I.
Retweet if you want me to get the biggest pop star on the planet – Justin Bieber – to contact you directly. He's a friend of mine. I have his phone number. And he will contact whoever I tell him to. Are you a beautiful girl? Maybe he will fall for you. You'll never know if this is true or not if you don't retweet it. Mind

* http://gor.mn/CuddleSpam

you, for some reason, this weird offer only applies to accounts that follow Nicky Paris.

Tweet 3 (Sent 7 May & 21 May 2012)[*]

@StealHisHeart

I'll DM Zayn, Niall, Liam, Louis, Harry, JB, Ed Sheeran + SELENA AND DEMI for u if you follow @TheNickyParis

Translation:

My account bio says 'Follow me if you adore those guys who are cute to you ♥' so it's probably safe to assume this account is aimed at teenage girls.
I am able to personally make direct contact with the individual members of the pop group, One Direction, the pop star, Justin Bieber, and the singer song-writer who might be credible but might not, nobody's quite sure since he started hanging out with the teenybopper types, Ed Sheeran. And I will do so on your behalf. But not just them, I will also contact actress/singer/one-time-Justin-Bieber-girlfriend, Selena Gomez – and the actress/singer/recently-announced-new-judge-on-the-US-X-Factor Demi Lovato. I can't explain how I am able to do this for you. All you need

* http://gor.mn/DMZaynSpam

> to know is that I will do it. But only if you follow Nicky
> Paris. It might look a bit strange – that someone with
> this degree of contact with the stars you idolise would
> use it as bait to persuade random strangers to follow
> someone else. But that's just the kind of guy I am.
> Quirky!

There were at least a dozen similarly brazen tweets from other accounts. I know they're transparent. But who are they aimed at? The teenage girls who are lost in a whirl of hormones and hysteria? The girls who've most completely fallen under the spell of Justin Bieber or One Direction or whichever new, doe-eyed stripling is next for the tattooist's chair, are surely the ones least likely to think rationally. They are *fans*. They are fanatics.

I know that I'm a chump at times. I'm a man in my 40s who sent a tweet to tease a teenager. I'm not proud of that. What the hell was I doing tabulating 23 of his accounts? Arranging them in numerical order, based on their total tweets? What was I thinking? It's only Twitter, for crying out loud. It's not important.

Except it is. For no reason other than we've decided it is. And it will continue to be until we snap out of it. How important is it? It's so important that a kid in New York was moved to send a quarter of a million tweets telling strangers to follow him, that's how important. The world told him that it was a measure of success. He believed them. Is that his fault or ours?

That said, the Bieber-bait strikes me as particularly ugly. The trade-off tweets were bad enough. All the you-follow-me-and-I'll-follow-you and if-you-retweet-me-five-times-I'll-retweet-you-back stuff is corrosive, sure, but if two people enter into such a deal, at least they're being honest with one another while they collude in being dishonest with the rest of us. But *this* stuff? There's not an ounce of honesty here. Offering teenage girls the thing they want most when you don't possess it is a cur's trick. Even if you are a teenage boy.

It's worth pointing out that time has passed. As I write this, Nicky appears to have gone more than a year spam-free. Maybe he's wiser. He is in his twenties, now, after all. In fact as he himself tweeted* in October 2013:

@TheNickyParis
Know that every time you post something on ANY
social networking site, someone is judging you.
Someone named me.

Wise words.**

* http://gor.mn/NPEveryTime
** A few weeks before this book went to print Nicky Paris changed his twitter name. And to make matters even more complicated, someone else seems to have started using the name @TheNickyParis. At least I'm pretty sure it's someone else. The account tweets Russian bon mots such as, 'почему я слушаю испанский рок, я даже не знаю о чем они поют' which, according to Google translate means, 'why I listen to Spanish rock, I do not even know what they sing' and 'путевка в лагерь образец' which means, 'stay in the camp sample.' Your guess is as good as mine.

CHAPTER 34

· · · · · · · · · · · ·

WHY DO THE PHONES IN HTC'S ADVERTS

ALL SHOW THE SAME TIME?

HTC are a Taiwanese firm who manufacture mobile phones.

My second favourite fact about HTC is that they were originally called the High Tech Computer Corporation. I like that name. If you were writing a Bond film in which the megalomaniac villain runs an apparently legitimate and not-at-all-evil company that later turns out to be nothing of the sort, you might call that company the High Tech Computer Corporation. But only in your first draft. You'd make a big note in the margin to come up with something less childish and a bit more convincing at a later date.

But that's only my second favourite HTC fact. My favourite HTC fact is this: in every advert I've ever seen for their phones, the time on the phone has always – and I mean *always* – been 10:08.

I'm not sure why – but I have a theory. To explain my theory, I need to take you back a few years.

At the age of eighteen I went to Manchester University to study mathematics. Or at least that's what it said on the forms. I don't know to what extent I really *wanted* to study mathematics. What I really *wanted* to do was leave home, spread my wings, try living in a big city and, y'know, find out who I was. A maths degree was just the flag of convenience under which I sailed.

I suppose it worked. I did find out who I was. I was someone who didn't want a maths degree. So I dropped out.

Officially I dropped out at the end of my second year but the truth is I stopped dropping in long before that. I don't think I attended a single lecture during that second year. It wasn't because I was a lazy, unmotivated student. It was because I was a hard-working, highly motivated, fledgling stand-up comic.

I'd started performing stand-up and I immediately knew that I'd found something I wanted to pursue. And in those days there was only one way of pursuing it. Spamming a quarter of a million people on Twitter wasn't an option. You just had to do as many gigs as possible.

There was only one comedy club in Manchester back then – and they wouldn't book an act more than twice in the same calendar year – so I had to travel further afield. I'd cheerfully spend five hours travelling just to do ten minutes here or fifteen minutes there. If I was lucky the promoter might pay for my train fare. But more often than not I was losing money in order to gain experience.

I needed the experience. I was *loving* the experience. No part of me ever considered saying, '*I'd love to do the gig … but I can't do a show in Luton on a Thursday night or I'll have to miss my Friday morning lecture on matrix functions … sorry …*'

But while I stopped going to any of my scheduled lectures, I did develop a habit of popping into lectures on completely unrelated subjects. Y'know, just for something to do. I'd just wander around the university campus until I saw a group of students filing into a lecture hall and then tag along for the ride. Or I'd accompany a friend who was studying philosophy for an afternoon if they told me their course was getting especially interesting. I didn't really care what the subject was – just so long as the lecture was conducted in English I figured it was worth giving it a go.

Even when the class was small enough for the tutor to notice my presence and query it, nobody really seemed to mind. I once joined a group of no more than a dozen students as they discussed a farce by the French playwright Georges Feydeau.

'I don't remember seeing you before?' The man in charge peered over the top of his glasses at me. 'What did you make of the play?'

'I haven't read it.' I shrugged. 'I'm a maths student. Sort of. I just thought this might be interesting.'

'And is it?'

'Yeah.'

It was his turn to shrug. 'Fair enough,' he said. And then he turned to the girl sitting to my left. He studied her features for a moment. 'Yes,' he said. 'I definitely know you. You're one of us. So, what did *you* make of it? What can a nineteenth-century French farce say to us about life in late twentieth-century Britain?'

If you've got some time to spare and live in a university town, I thoroughly recommend doing a bit of lecture-surfing. It's more stimulating than most daytime TV and you never know what weird knowledge you might soak up along the way.

For example, it was in one of these illicit lectures, more than twenty years ago, that I first heard about something called the *10:08 Rule Of Advertising*. It's stayed with me ever since.

I don't remember what degree course it was supposed to be a part of, I just know that the lecture concerned various ways in which we are manipulated by shopkeepers and salesmen in their efforts to part us from our cash. The lecturer discussed the various techniques used by supermarkets – pumping out the smell of freshly baked bread, for example – and the way in which shopping malls are deliberately designed to disorientate and confuse you in order to make you dawdle, browse and, ultimately, buy something you weren't actually looking for. (It's known as The Gruen Transfer and is named after one of the pioneers of these dark arts, the Austrian architect, Victor Gruen.) He discussed the 99p effect – you *really* are more likely to buy something if it's priced at £9.99, £19.99 or, for that matter, £999.99 instead of £10, £20 or £1,000 respectively. We all like to think we're not taken in by that one. But we are. We all are.*

Much of the lecture concerned stuff I was already vaguely aware of but even when it was new to me it all chimed so fully with my own experience of the world that I knew it just had to be true. Apart from one thing: something our lecturer dubbed the *10:08 Rule Of Advertising*.

The *10:08* rule concerns the selling of clocks and watches. Apparently, they sell better when the hands are pointing up and out, like a flattened, squashed, capital V. The theory is that it resembles a smile. And for some reason, we want our clocks to be happy.

A clearly delighted clock

So watch and clockmakers routinely display their merchandise looking pleased to see you and for reasons

---

* My publishers certainly think you'll fall for it. You can find some proof on the back cover of this book.

that nobody really understands, the most common time chosen is 10:08 rather than, say, 1:51 or the more perfectly symmetrical 10:10. (Theory has it that we grow suspicious if it's 10:10 exactly. It's *too* precise. It makes us sense human intervention. As a result we feel manipulated and so our brains un-manipulate themselves accordingly. But at 10:08? Well, then it's just a good-natured, happy-go-lucky timepiece with a lopsided grin.)

I remember sitting in the lecture theatre doubting this 10:08 business. After all, I'd bought watches before. I'd browsed the Argos catalogue. I'd walked past the kitchen clock display in John Lewis. I'd never noticed any ten-oh-eightness before. Surely I'd have spotted something like that, wouldn't I?

I think that initial sense of doubt goes a long way towards explaining quite why it's stayed with me in the way it has. Because for more than twenty years it has been impossible for me to see a clock advertised for sale and not check to see whether or not it's 'smiling'. And they invariably are. In advertising-land, clocks really do look happy. The 10:08 rule, it seems, holds true.

But surely that can't be the reason for HTC using it in their adverts, can it? I can just about accept that – on some subliminal level, at least – *this* clock face has a 'smile':

But somehow, when it's translated into a digital display, it stops being quite so easy to discern:

It just looks a bit more, y'know, *like some numbers*.

Is it possible, do you think, that someone in the marketing department of HTC mobile phones *actually* thinks that 10:08 is just an inherently happy time? Of course it *could* just be a coincidence. Maybe the photo shoot for their first phone advert started at 10 a.m. and the magical shot was taken just eight minutes later? How long can it take to photograph a phone after all? It doesn't have mood swings or a change of costume. Nobody's insisting on touching up its make-up. It's just a bloody phone. So maybe that's all it is: a photo that just happened to be taken at 10:08.

But that seems unlikely. And even if it is true, for the

same time to have appeared on *every* HTC ad since would involve someone from the company saying, '*Hey, y'know that photo, the one we used in the ad? Yeah. I liked it a lot. But – and I know you might think this is weird – the thing I liked most about it was the time. I don't know why. I just thought it* looked *good. So, um … could we always photograph the phones at 10:08 in future? Thanks.*'

Doesn't it seem more likely that someone in the marketing department has simply accepted the 10:08 rule as fact? If nobody had ever explained to you why it's supposed to work for analogue clocks would you just assume it was true for *all* clocks?

There are plenty of 'facts' in my head that I've never questioned. Frothing milk to make a cappuccino? *Always* use a stainless steel jug. I've no idea what science informs that 'fact' and I've *never* tried frothing milk in a jug made out of pyrex or plastic. I've just taken it on faith to be true and got on with it.

Folding egg whites? *Always* use a large metal spoon. I guess there *must* be a reason for that. It's just never occurred to me to doubt it.

Maybe the HTC marketing executive responsible for this decision is similarly accepting. Maybe they think the numbers one, zero, zero and eight work through some kind of witchcraft? Maybe they've never so much as wondered why it works and just bought the idea that it does.

In a way, I hope that's what it is. Because that would

mean that every time they advertise their phones, they also advertise their own stupidity. And when I think of it in those terms, weirdly the time 10:08 *actually* does start to make me happy.

CHAPTER 35

. . . .

IF YOU'RE GOING TO PRETEND YOU'RE A PROPER MAGAZINE AT LEAST MAKE AN EFFORT

O ut of all the print publications in the UK – that's every newspaper and every magazine – which do you think is the most read? I would have guessed the *Sun*. Or maybe the *Daily Mail*? Surely every copy of *Metro* is read by six or seven people a day thanks to their unique abandoned-on-public-transport distribution system, so maybe that's in the running?

Apparently not. As of November 2012 the most read printed publication in the UK was – drum roll, please – *Tesco Magazine*.

I know. You probably need a moment to think about this. I know I did.

How are you feeling? It's a shock, isn't it? If you're struggling to believe me, this is how Cedar Communications – the company that produces *Tesco Magazine* – reported the results on their website:*

* http://gor.mn/NRSmostread

Tesco magazine has overtaken the Sun to claim the title of most read printed publication in the UK, according to the latest report from the National Readership Survey (NRS).

Following year-on-year growth of eight per cent during the period (October 2011 – September 2012) *Tesco magazine* has a readership of 7·221m, exceeding all national press (dailies and Sundays) and magazines.

The NRS report shows the *Sun* has a readership of 7·1m. Tesco's competitor *Asda magazine* has 6m readers, while *Sainsbury's magazine* has 3·4m and *Your M&S* has 3·7m. *Tesco magazine* is published by content marketing agency Cedar.

Prior to the report, Tesco held the title of the UK's most-read women's magazine, trumping other supermarket and newsstand publications.

And *this* is how they describe the magazine:

The magazine is focused around three pillars – food, family and living. It packs in ideas and features on everything customers need to enjoy great food experiences, from planning the weekly shop to cooking nutritious meals to share with friends and family.

Well, you can't argue with their three pillars, can you? Food. Family. Living. They've covered all the bases there. It's certainly true that your family needs food if they're to remain living. Not that you need me to tell you that.

Even if you've never seen the magazine, I'm sure you have a pretty good idea of what to expect. You know it's going to look like a regular lifestyle magazine. You know it will contain the usual features and articles – little domestic tips and tricks, recipes, interior design suggestions, relationship advice and so on. But you also know in what ways it will be different. You know that it will be free. And you know that it will be Tescofied.

You know that reading a copy won't be quite like reading a regular magazine because you know that every now and then there will be a Tesco-shaped bump in the road to remind you what it really is: an advert. It doesn't *really* exist to tell you how to upcycle an old cardigan. It's not really published in order to offer you advice on how to talk to your teen. It might do those things. But they're not its raison d'être. It exists to shill for Tesco.

And there's nothing wrong with that. At least it's honest. And I'm sure most people who pick up the magazine take what it says with a pinch of salt as a result. We know what we're reading and we understand that a tacit deal has been struck: it's free … but everything comes from a Tesco-y point of view. If you give a newsagent 86p for a copy of *Take a Break* magazine you're entitled to expect a more independent view (and, more than likely, some horrible stories about a bigamist stepdad with a violent past that's come back to haunt him) but a free read is a free read and you understand that it's a propaganda sheet of sorts.

In truth, I think most of us regard it – and others of its kind – as sort of *pretend* magazines. Imagine there's a copy of *Tesco Magazine* on your kitchen table. Imagine you're asking your partner to pass it to you. Role-play it in your mind. '*Can you pass me that copy of* Tesco Magazine?' It's almost impossible to say without putting the word *magazine* in some imaginary inverted commas, isn't it? Because your brain knows that *magazine* is the only word for it ... but your gut is telling you that it's not one. Not really. So your tone of voice puts it in inverted commas and what you're really saying is, '*Can you pass me that copy of Tesco's sort-of magazine-type-thing?*'

But even if it is a pretend magazine ... could they not try pretending a little better? Could they not try and be a little more subtle?

I'll show you what I mean with an example. The headline for this particular article is '**How to plan a long car journey**'. Beneath it is a large picture of a pretty woman – she looks a bit like Cameron Diaz. She's leaning out of a car window, has a pair of sunglasses resting on her head and a big smile on her face. Beneath the picture, the sub-headline explains the article's brief: '*If you're making the most of the UK this summer, here are some tips to get you on the road.*'

So you know what to expect, right? Stay alert. Take breaks. Stay hydrated. (Guess who sells bottled water.) Check your tyres. Take some snacks. (Might we interest you in some snacks?) Keep the kids entertained. Have their favourite CDs in the car. (What's that? Yes, yes, we do sell CDs.) And so on.

Isn't that the form? Surely that's how these things are written. You write the article you would write for a normal magazine and then scan through it looking for opportunities to Tesco it up. Don't you?

Apparently not. They came up with three tips. Just three! They were as follows:

Plan your route in advance

Make sure you know where you can fill up on petrol. You can collect Clubcard points on Tesco fuel and if you use your Clubcard Credit Card, you'll collect even more points. (Available to UK residents, over-18s only, subject to status. Excludes Esso fuel.)

Keep the kids entertained

How about playing backseat bingo? Make a bingo sheet for everyone with pictures of things you might see on your car journey. The first one to spot them all wins!

Consider taking out breakdown cover

This will help you get back on the road quickly if anything goes wrong across the UK and Europe. Tesco Breakdown Cover offers four levels of cover and is provided by RAC Motoring Services and/or RAC Insurance Limited.

And that's it, is it? Just the three 'tips'? Surely this is the minimum level of effort required on their part, isn't it? I mean, three ideas just doesn't feel like a list. Not really. What this list amounts to is a pub conversation with the know-it-all bloke who turns out to know nothing at all.

'Hello, young man, the bar steward tells me you're planning a long drive soon. I happen to be a bit of a motoring expert ... would you like the benefit of my advice?'

'Really? Yes. That's fabulous ... thank you ... I'm all ears ...'

'Well, I can sell you some cheap petrol if you're interested ...'

'Sounds good.'

'All you need to do is plan your route to take in my locations.'

'Are they on the motorway?'

'Um ... no.'

'Oh. Only, it's a long drive, I don't really want to get snarled up on some ring road looking for petrol ...'

'OK, OK ... well, I can do you a deal on breakdown cover if you fancy it.'

'Right. Um ... I'll bear that in mind ... but what about advice? For the long drive?'

'Oh that ... yeah ... oh, I dunno ... bingo ... something, y'know ... like those *I Spy* books ... yeah ... do that.'

'Oh. OK. How do you mean exactly?'

'Well, y'know, you should make some bingo cards. Pictures of stuff that you cross off when you see them.'

'I see. Do you mean we should draw them? Or cut pictures out of a magazine or ...?'

'Oh, whatever.'

'Well, what do you do when you do it with *your* kids?'

'I've never … really … um … it's not really a thing I do …'

'Oh. OK. Well … what about safety? I mean … y'know … it's a long drive …'

'Pffft. Not really my area, mate.' He sups from his pint. 'Look, do you want to buy some petrol or don't you?'

Chapter 36

· · · · · · · · · · · ·

START YOUR AD WRONG

With the near constant flow of information in our world it stands to reason that we'll all encounter a hefty slice of nonsense. Some of that nonsense exists because people aren't trying and some of it exists because they have to try so hard just to get our attention that clarity soon goes out the window. But some of it is nonsense just because it is nonsense.

Advertisers have to try and make a case for their product being better. Better than it used to be. Better than its rivals. But not every product can constantly improve. Surely some things have been perfected by now. Nobody's going to invent a *better* paper clip any time soon and I'm pretty sure mankind nailed the teaspoon some time ago.

But there are some products that people refuse to accept have reached their acme. I don't care how many different pieces of coloured plastic and rubber knobbly bits they try and integrate into the design, I'm not convinced that toothbrushes are getting better. I'm pretty sure the deodorant I sprayed under my armpits as a teenager was just as effective as the one I sprayed under my armpits this morning, too.

But you can't tell the manufacturers that. They won't have it. They want us to believe that things are getting better and some poor sod has to come up with advertising campaigns that make the case. It's an impossible case to make. Of course they produce nonsense.

Let's have a look at a couple of examples.

With an arrogant swipe of his right hand, a bare-chested man knocks a handful of bottles, cans and canisters from the shelf in front of his bathroom mirror. Maybe it's not his bathroom? He's making a hell of a mess if it's not. But it's highly unlikely to be a friend's bathroom. Nobody would treat their friend's stuff with such disdain. Somebody's going to have to pick that up. The only explanation really is that it's a hotel. But those products look full size. Hmm. Maybe they'd been left behind by the people before him? Maybe he's knocking them off the shelf in anger that his room hasn't been cleaned properly? Whatever the reason, he replaces them with the one product he requires. A can of Right Guard deodorant. I know it's Right Guard because the camera lingers on the pack shot. From the pack shot we cut back to the six-pack shot as the shirtless man sprays the deodorant at his armpit. The slate-grey bathroom behind him looks huge. It must be a fancy hotel.

While all that happens, an urgent, masculine voice-over declaims, '*Start your day right with new Right Guard Extreme, the first 48-hour antiperspirant with antibacterial silver molecules that fight body odour at its source for 48 hours.*'

Whenever this ad came on the TV I'd turn the volume down, convinced that if I listened closely I would hear the nation exploding as one in rage. Surely other people were watching the same channel as me! Surely I wasn't the only person in the land watching that commercial! Why weren't there gasps of incredulity up and down the land?

I started asking friends if they'd seen it, just to check that I wasn't imagining it. I wasn't. When their memories were nudged they'd recall it. But only vaguely. Most, it seemed, had never really listened to it. They hadn't really taken it in. '*I sort of tune out when the ads are on,*' was a pretty common explanation.

The ad makers must know that we want to avoid their work. Maybe they're not really trying to communicate with us directly? Maybe we're not supposed to take in the whole thing? Maybe they're just hoping an image, a word, a moment of some kind will lodge itself in our subconscious. That's all it needs. When you're in the shops, looking at all the different cans of deodorant, lined up side by side, somewhere at the back of your mind, a thought, a mood, a tone of voice, a *something* will be there just gently guiding your hand a little, this way or that, to pick up the Right Guard. You don't know why. But it just *feels* right. Better. Possibly. Kind of.

So maybe I'm the fool for actually watching it! For actually expecting it to make sense! If you ask me, it starts going wrong from the third word.

'*Start your day right …*'

Hang on. This is a *48-hour* antiperspirant. If it works for 48 hours, surely the ad should say '*Start two days right*'. But then that wouldn't be right either. Wearing a deodorant for two days means not taking a shower, so really it should say '*Start two days wrong*'. But you can't really call a product Right Guard Extreme if it's for starting two days wrong so they'd be better off calling it Extremely Wrong Guard.

Yes. I think my rewrite makes much more sense: '*Start two days wrong with new Extremely Wrong Guard, the first 48-hour antiperspirant with antibacterial silver molecules that fight body odour at its source for 48 hours.*'

What kind of pointless improvement is it to make a deodorant last 48 hours? If you know anyone who's using a deodorant every other day you need to have a quiet word. Which will be tricky because you won't want to get too close to the smelly sod.

They can't really be recommending that you use it for 48 hours, can they? Surely what it really means is '*stronger-than-normal-24-hour antiperspirant*' and what *that* really means is '*spray for really smelly bastards*' but they can't call it that because nobody's going to go up to the counter in Superdrug with a can of Really-Smelly-Bastards deodorant are they?

And now you can buy 72-hour and even 96-hour deodorants too. (It's strange, isn't it? How the 'improvements' come in precise 24-hour slots of extra efficacy?)

Is a 96-hour deodorant better than a 72-hour better than a 48, better than a 24? Not if you're going to spray it on in the morning and wash it off that night it's not. It's like boasting that you've made a pacemaker that's guaranteed to keep working for five years after the transplant patient has died. (And then 'improving' it by making a new one that will go on for ten years after … and so on.)

Meanwhile …

A luminescent jellyfish propels itself upwards, its whole body throbbing once and then twice. There is music. Just a beat at first. A drum. Or maybe a human heart. One, two.

As the beat continues – three, four – we see speeded-up footage of New York cabs arriving at a busy intersection on a dark night. The lights are red. The cabs pause. The lights are green. The cabs drive. The city is breathing. Five, six.

'A pulse …' says a reassuring voice as we cut to a model striding up the runway at a swanky fashion show. Flashbulbs flash – seven, eight. What else could flashbulbs do? There's no time for such thoughts. The beat is gathering pace. The voice continues: '*... the whole world has a pulse ...*'

A field of corn moves with the breeze – nine, ten – a yellow cloth buffs a shiny black leather shoe – eleven, twelve. Quicker still. A lawn sprinkler, sprinkles – thirteen, fourteen – a footballer bounces a ball on his head – fifteen, sixteen, seventeen, eighteen – and then there's a crescendo of sorts.

The screen is white. Godly. Climactic. It shines bright. This was the moment we've been building towards.

'*Now ...*' says the voice. An object emerges from the centre of the screen: is it a holy relic? '*... so does a toothbrush.*'

Oh.

It's a toothbrush.

'*New Oral-B Pulsar ...*'

There's more to the ad* but I can't get past this opening line. It is simply impossible for my brain to unpack it.

'*A pulse. The whole world has a pulse. Now ... so does a toothbrush.*'

What? What does this mean?

'*A pulse.*' OK. Yes. I know what a pulse is.

'*The whole world has a pulse.*' So, everything in the

---

* Shortly before publication, the English language version of this ad disappeared from the internet ... but I found a Spanish language version: http://gor.mn/ToothPulsar

whole wide world has a pulse, does it? I'm not sure I agree with you on that … but go on, I'll entertain the notion.

'*Now … so does a toothbrush.*'

Whoa there. *Now? Now?* So a toothbrush *didn't* have a pulse until *now?* But *everything else* did? So when you said the *whole* world has a pulse … you didn't really mean the *whole* world. You meant the whole world *apart* from a toothbrush. So the toothbrush is the *last* object on planet earth to finally get on board with the pulse thing? Really?

I mean. Really? A desk? A shed? A paving stone? A dead pig? They all have pulses? But a toothbrush doesn't? Until *now*!

Was this advert made by drunk people?

Again, I can rewrite it to make it make sense. Here you go:

'*A pulse. Some things in the world have a pulse. And now, a toothbrush is one of those things.*'

How's that? Better? Good.

Chapter 37

· · · · · · · · · · · · ·

JUST BECAUSE YOU CAN CON A COMPUTER IT DOESN'T MEAN THAT YOU SHOULD

Flickr is a website for photographers. It's a place to upload photos. You can keep them private if you just want a place to store your work or you can share them with a select band of people to whom you've granted permission. Or you can make them publicly available to anyone and everyone. You can gather them in sets of your own or add them to public groups based on almost any theme you can imagine. A group exists solely for pictures of dogs in pools.* And if that sounds a bit broad, well, there's another devoted to pictures of people with bits of their anatomy wrapped in tin foil.** And if you can't find a group for something, then you can always set one up. If you prefer you can ignore all that and just leave your stuff in a disorganised jumble – it's up to you. You can comment on others' photos and they can comment on yours. You can 'favourite' the shots you like most. Or the ones you'd

---

* http://gor.mn/FlickrPoolDogs
** http://gor.mn/FlickrFoil

like to come back to another day for some other reason. Whatever works for you. I like Flickr. I'm not the only one. It plays host to what is, I think, an unusually passionate community of users. Every time Flickr tweaks the design or tinkers with the interface, the forums are plunged into uproar. '*It was perfect before! You changed it! How could you! Everything is terrible now. Why do you hate us so? Go to hell!*' Etc, etc, etc.

One of Flickr's features is called Explore. Explore is a page where they show the 'most interesting photos on Flickr'. I guess it's a sort of shop window for the site. A place where anyone can idly browse with the reasonable expectation that what they're seeing won't be terrible.

Over the years I have got used to seeing the occasional Flickr-user struck down with a bad case of Explore-fever. The disease develops in two stages and the symptoms are easy to spot.

Stage One: the user is convinced that their own photos are better than some of those they're seeing in Explore. '*Whoever's picking these photos for Explore has lousy taste*,' they think. '*Why do none of my photos make it? It must be broken!*'

At this point people patiently explain that nobody is picking and choosing the photos. Between one and two million photos are being uploaded every day. Looking at them all would be impossible, let alone trying to select 'the best' of them. It is selected by an algorithm of some kind.

How many views it has had and how many people have made it a favourite. Or passed a comment. How many groups is it in? How many sets is it in? How much metadata is associated with it? Have you added it to a map? Somehow, all of this information is measured and some secret formula is used to arrive as a measure of 'interestingness'.

This knowledge is sometimes enough to cure a mild case of Explore-fever. It's just computers doing what computers do. There are millions of photos. Only 500 are in Explore at any one time. Of course they're not selected by people. Of course a computer can't make a value judgement about the composition of a photo. It doesn't know how many of the photos contain cats. It doesn't know how many are sunsets. It isn't *looking at the photos*. Only at the data. You can't read an insult into not making the cut because the cut wasn't based on any qualitative judgements. Relax.

But for many, this is not enough. Their illness will rapidly proceed to Stage Two.

Stage Two: even though the user now knows that whether or not a photo is in Explore says nothing about the quality of that photo, they are still determined to get their work into Explore. The knowledge that it is essentially meaningless hasn't put them off. If anything, it has spurred them on. '*If there's an algorithm,*' they think, '*then I can crack it! I'll work out exactly what combination of statistics are required and make sure all of my photos achieve it! That prize*

– that prize that I now know means nothing at all – will be mine!'

There are groups devoted to cracking the code. People trade favourites with one another and discuss tactics. Tactics! Tactics to con a computer into liking a photo it cannot see!

As far as I know, there is no known cure for Stage Two Explore-fever. But this is just a microcosm of an illness that is striking all across the internet. Wherever things are measured, rated and compared by computers, people are out there trying to game the system.

How many friends have you got? How many likes did you get? How many followers do you have? How many favourites? How many views? All across the internet, people are trying to find ways of artificially improving these meaningless numbers.

Of course it's one thing when people are trying to con a computer into thinking they're a photographer of note … but all systems can be gamed and sometimes the motivation is profit.

I have a blog. One day I was surprised to see someone with the username *angelosam123*[*] leaving a comment on my blog. The comment read as follows:

angelosam123:
Solicitors High Wycombe for commercial law solicitors <u>*solicitors High Wycombe*</u>*.*

[*] http://gor.mn/angelosam123

This would be an odd comment to leave on any blog. Even if the blog post in question had been about solicitors and/or High Wycombe, it would be odd because it isn't a coherent sentence. It's lacking something. Verbs, mainly.

Of course it goes without saying that my blog wasn't about solicitors. Nor was it *about* High Wycombe. It *mentioned* High Wycombe. In passing. It mentioned 30 or 40 other towns too. It was no more a blog post about High Wycombe than this is a book about badger-themed glove puppets.

So why was that comment there? Why was someone looking at my blog and leaving a comment that would be meaningless to any pair of human eyes? It wasn't posted in the hope that a person would look at it. It was posted in order to be seen by a computer. It existed in order to try and game the system.

The final three words in that comment were a link. If you clicked on it you would find yourself at the website CurzonGreen.co.uk. They're a firm of solicitors. I'm sure you can guess where they're based.

But *angelosam123* wasn't posting the comment hoping that someone might one day read my blog, stumble on the link, click through to Curzon Green and then engage their services to help with their divorce or some conveyancing. It was just there to try and fool Google. Just as Flickr doesn't have anyone looking at every photo, so Google doesn't have anyone reading every web page. When you search for something on Google the first results aren't the first results because they've been handpicked by an expert Google employee as the most likely to be of use to you. They're the first results because an algorithm has put them there.

Many different factors are taken into account by that algorithm. Amongst them are such things as i) how many links there are to the page in question and ii) what words are used in those links.

By leaving that comment, *angelosam123* was attempting to improve Curzon Green's search-engine ranking. *Angelosam123* trying to con Google into putting Curzon Green's website nearer the top of the results for anyone using the search terms 'High Wycombe solicitor'.

Why would a firm of solicitors be spamming my blog? Is that seemly behaviour for a solicitor? Wouldn't taking an ad in the local paper be a bit more, y'know ... honest?

Well, Curzon Green weren't. I doubt they even knew it was happening. Certainly, when I emailed them to tell them about it they appeared to be suitably embarrassed. If I was them, I'd have been embarrassed too. It's a bloody stupid way for a solicitor to advertise. If I was Mr Curzon* or Mr Green and I discovered someone had been advertising my firm in that manner I'd be mortified. Blog-spam is where you expect to see an advert for dodgy Viagra or a seedy escort agency, not a Buckinghamshire solicitors. It's like advertising your firm by putting a postcard in a Soho phone box next to all the hookers.

---

* I don't actually know if Mr Curzon exists, but I did speak to one of their Mr Greens and he was very helpful.

Blog-spam isn't meant to be seen by human eyes, but if someone *does* see it, they're not necessarily going to hold you in high regard. And solicitors are the kind of people who rely on high regard.

No, Curzon Green hadn't posted that comment themselves. What they'd done is employ a search engine optimisation company to try and help them build a web presence for their newly established office. The company in question were iSEOmarketing.co.uk ... who are also known as SEO4Solicitors.com ... who are also known as Stephen Moore.

I have very little good to say for those who work in search engine optimisation. Maybe I'm doing them a terrible disservice. Maybe it's a hugely valuable industry that's added to the net happiness of our world – and perhaps to the happiness of our 'net – in ways I'm just not sophisticated enough to comprehend. All I know is that I've encountered a dozen or more of its practitioners and they've all had the whiff of snake-oil about them.

It's an industry that knows its clients don't really understand how Google and Bing and the other search engines work. '*Don't worry your pretty little heads,*' they say, '*we'll get you to Google's front page, no trouble at all. And don't worry, it's all above board!*'

The industry has a phrase for what you and I might call 'above board'. Good, ethical SEO behaviour is called 'White Hat SEO'. The more unsavoury tactics are called 'Black Hat SEO'.

White Hat SEO focuses on a human audience. It tries to influence search engines by creating content that is relevant in a way that real people will understand. Leave a comment on a blog by all means, but do it on a blog post that is pertinent. Do it honestly – in your own name – and add a link that you believe is helpful. There's nothing wrong with that. It's when the comment is irrelevant to the host blog, when it makes no attempt to make sense for a human audience, when it simply adds to the overwhelming tide of garbage that is clogging up the internet, that I have a problem with it. Because its very existence is a selfish 'fuck you' to everyone else. '*I know this comment-section exists so that people can discuss this blog,*' says the Black Hat SEO, '*but sod that, I'm not interested in anybody else.*'

It's like joining a book group, turning up at the meeting and – when asked for your thoughts on the novel – shouting, '*Cheap double glazing, quality garage doors, Gravesend, Kent! Garage doors, Gravesend, Kent!*' and then leaving.

There's so much of this nonsense about that any individual example appears trivial. It's just a comment! Nothing to get worked up about. Just delete it and move on. But you could make the same argument about litter and I'd still think you were a selfish twonk for dropping your crisp packet in the street. Imagine how much nicer the internet would be if *none* of that pointless scum was floating on top of it? Imagine that the internet was just you and me and everyone else using it for our own purposes.

If every page of the world wide web was something created by a *person* in the hope that other *people* would see it and none of it was created by weasely nerds, trying to fool computers, wouldn't that be ... y'know ... better?

We are stupid and we are wise. We are right and we are wrong. We are entertaining and we are educational and boring and misinformed. We are caring and callous and silly and serious and ridiculous – always, *always* ridiculous – but we are real. Isn't the sum total of what we have to contribute to the world wide web enough for Google to be picking its way through without SEOs adding a layer of guff to the mix in the hope that its judgement can be skewed?

The SEO4Solicitors.com website made for interesting reading. They had a guarantee:

OUR GUARANTEE

At SEO4Solicitors.com our goal is to represent and promote Solicitors/Law Firm throughout the UK on Google and Bing search engines to achieve the highest ranking.

We will achieve this via ethical 'white hat' optimisation methods and techniques.

And a testimonial from Curzon Green:

'The SEO services were well explained and useful. I could not have asked for a better service.'

Curzon Green Solicitors

Although both were taken off the site within a few hours of me questioning their veracity.

I did call Stephen Moore to ask why his company were spamming and he seemed like a nice chap. A chirpy Scouser, he was, I think, genuinely apologetic. He was also frustratingly cagey about the details: 'Look, I don't want to say too much in case you make me look stupid, but you're right, it shouldn't have happened.'

The facts of the matter are that he subcontracts some of what he does to people in India and because English isn't their first language, mistakes get made.

I wonder if that rather unglamorous side of the SEO business is explained to their clients? I bet Curzon Green thought they were paying for some whizz-bang technology and cutting-edge computer know-how, not for some poor person in Delhi to do some piece-work typing spam. It's the Wizard of Oz. Pull back the curtain and you find it's not a wizard at all ... it's just a bloke typing.

Of course, leaving spammy comments on blogs isn't the limit of an SEO's activity. One of Moore's other clients are a firm of Liverpool solicitors called Cobley's LLP who have the web domain easylaw.co.uk. Just as someone with the username *angelosam123* was spreading links on behalf of Curzon Green, so someone with the username *Glenn Jacob** had been spreading links to Cobley's. They sometimes did so by leaving comments

* http://gor.mn/GlennJacob

on blogs, but have also written an article that they've published on several sites. The article is titled 'Hiring a litigation expert is necessary to win–win!!' and at the time of writing I've found it on at least a dozen sites, including zimbio.com, hotklix.com, folkd.com, hellocoton.fr, yooarticles.net and yanghew.com. The opening paragraph reads as follows:

> The most agreeable person on Earth even comes to a situation in the entire life span when he needs to hire a legal professional. There may be varied reasons to hire skilled legal counsel. If you're obtaining a <u>divorce Liverpool</u>, suffering from family disputes, judicial proceeding, estate matters or something else, you would be looking for solicitors or lawyers for the same. Hiring a professional is often a good decision to keep unwanted burden off of your shoulders. If you are not a wrongfully savvy person then likelihood is that you will not be able to plan your stuff accordingly.

This obviously isn't the writing of a native English speaker. But then, I don't think it's really the writing of someone who's learning English as a second language either. Surely only a computer running automatic translation software would come up with the words '*The most agreeable person on Earth even comes to a situation in the entire life span when he needs to hire a legal professional*'. One can only wonder how many languages it has been filtered through. Maybe the original article was written by someone else in English and translating it in and out of various languages is a way of disguising its theft?

I suppose for the most part you know what it's trying to say. Apart from the phrase, '*If you are not a wrongfully savvy person.*' I've stared at that clause for fifteen minutes and I still can't quite unravel its meaning. And what is the word '*Liverpool*' doing in the third sentence? '*If you're obtaining a divorce Liverpool ...*' It's obviously there because '*divorce Liverpool*' is one of the search terms they're trying to work for them.

If the lawyers from Cobley's – which, by all accounts, is a very professional and established firm of solicitors – were to read that article, do you think they'd think, '*Yep ... that's* exactly *how we'd like our company to appear online. Anyone reading that would clearly see that we're the firm for them. Unless they're wrongfully savvy. Or something*'? If not, why does it exist? Couldn't someone from Cobley's cobble together an article that made some sense, something that showed them as they'd like to be seen? Why not ask them to do that and then spend your time cutting and pasting that around the internet instead of this auto-translata-dross? Would that really be so much work?

If you were searching online for a solicitor – in High Wycombe, Liverpool or anywhere else for that matter – who would you hope to find at the top of the results? Would you want the firm that had been most discussed by real people online or the one that had paid a firm to generate fake chatter? Wouldn't a world without *angelo-sam123*, *Glenn Jacob* and all the other fake names created by all the other SEO companies to generate all the other tosh that's clogging up the internet's arteries be a bit more true and level? A bit more ours. And a bit less theirs?

CHAPTER 38

- - - - - - - - - - -

WHEN NOBODY BATS AN EYE AT AN ADVERT FOR AN ADVERT, SOMETHING SOMEWHERE MUST BE WRONG

Up until now when I've written about advertising I've assumed a certain widespread cynicism exists towards it. It stands to reason, doesn't it? Advertising exists to try and persuade us to spend money and it's wise to be at least a little suspicious of such things.

But there is an exception. The people of Britain have been sucked into a weird mass delusion. It happens in mid-November and, if you read a newspaper, watch television, listen to the radio or engage in any kind of social media it is impossible to avoid. We have decided that the launch of the John Lewis Christmas ad is an event.

Even the fact that we acknowledge its '*launch*' seems at odds with the way in which we normally view advertising. Advertising is considered an intrusion; a thing we try to avoid if we can. But as Christmas approaches, a high-street retail giant has acquired the power to melt our cynicism. Instead of regarding their ad as a minor inconvenience, people actually go out of their way to watch it. Hundreds of thousands of people look it up on YouTube because they don't want to run the risk of missing out! You can't miss it. You won't be able to join in with the conversation at work on Monday morning if you haven't seen it and while you were planning on watching *X Factor* on Saturday and it's almost certain to be shown during at least one of those breaks, you can't really afford to take that chance!

People get so excited about it you'd think JK Rowling was launching a Harry Potter edition iPad on centre court during Wimbledon fortnight. By 2019, I fully expect to see people camping out overnight – on John Lewis deckchairs, natch – to be first in line for special preview screenings.

Of course John Lewis gleefully hype the anticipation at every turn. In 2013, they even produced a teaser ad that was shown on the Wednesday night to let us know that the main event was only a couple of days away. How have we come to this? They're advertising their advert! And instead of cocking a snook at them for the ridiculousness of it all, we're buying into it! A two-minute ad for a department store is being treated as though it's the latest release from Quentin Taran-bloody-tino!

'*I wonder what they'll do this year?*' ask columnists everywhere. '*Will it be as good as last year?*' they ponder.

Why are we treating it with such reverence and import? In what way is that ad *important* to you?

'*It's a tradition,*' say the style pages. '*In many ways, it's the real start of the festive season.*'

Sod off! It is no such thing. It's not a tradition. If it *was* a tradition you'd have fond memories of the John Lewis Christmas ads of your childhood. And you don't. You don't because they only started making them in 2007! How have they got their hooks into us so quickly? By 2011, their ad, titled 'The Long Wait' (and, by the way, why the hell does an advert need a bloody title?), had the chattering classes chattering. Traditions – actual traditions – grow and develop over time. They are handed down from generation to generation. They are not made by ad agencies in just five goes.

Last December I genuinely heard someone say, '*Well, it just wouldn't be Christmas without the John Lewis ad, would it?*'

Yes. Yes, it would. I know. I survived 36 Christmases without a John Lewis ad and while my memories of the first few are patchy, the one thing that nobody ever complained about was how un-Christmassy Christmas was.

I don't hate all advertising. I don't think the whole industry is malign. I'm much too wishy-washy a soul to have opinions as clear cut as that. There's nothing about the John Lewis Christmas ads themselves that upset me. It's our reaction to them that's so unsettling. It's the about turn in our nation's psyche that unnerves me.

Watching Britain go weak at the knees *in anticipation* of a commercial just doesn't seem right. It makes me feel like I'm in one of those zombie films: I've woken up one morning to find everyone else looking pretty much as normal … just a little glassy-eyed, a bit subservient. At the end of the day, unconditionally opening your arms to an advertiser just isn't British!

CHAPTER 39

· · · · · · · · · · · ·

IF WE'RE SUPPOSED TO BELIEVE IN PRETEND PEOPLE, WE HAVE TO LET PRETEND PEOPLE LIVE IN THE REAL WORLD

Sometimes I find myself telling people that I used to live in New York. As the words fall from my lips I always wince because I know it's not true. It's not a lie either. It's just the phrase '*Oh yeah ... I used to live in New York*' is writing a cheque that my life experience can't really cash.

To say you *lived* overseas suggests a life of adventure, achievement or privilege. When British people talk about 'that time they lived in New York', they mean they spent a year there as part of a student exchange programme when they were younger, or that their high-flying career in banking saw them posted to the New York office for three years or that a wealthy relative with a New York base put them up every summer when they were a teenager. To say you 'lived' somewhere is to say you had a home there. A life there. I have never had any of those things in New York.

The longest I've spent there is three months. I've done that twice. On both occasions I was there for work. On both occasions I was staying in rented apartments. Neither apartment was a place I considered home. They were places to stay. Ramshackle, make-do places with unreliable hot water supplies. I never paid a utility bill. I only ever paid rent. If your name isn't on the electricity bill I don't think it's really your home.

I never felt like I was living there. I always felt like I was away from home. But at the same time, I wasn't on holiday. I wasn't staying in hotels. So I'm not lying when I say I lived there. I did. I just didn't, y'know, *live* there.

Three months is too long for it to feel like a break. But not long enough to establish a life. Not long enough to put down roots. It's something in between. In the context of a year it's hugely significant. In the context of a life, it's a mere blip. But it happened and sometimes a conversation steers me to a point where it would be weird not to mention it and so the phrase slips out ... always followed, a few moments later, by apologetic sub-clauses and codicils as I pull the rug from under myself and do my best to set it in its proper, more humble, context.

Still, my time spent not-quite-living-in New York has had a lasting effect on me. One of the more unexpected effects has been the way in which it has marred my enjoyment of American movies and TV shows. Especially where phone numbers are concerned.

I recognise a Manhattan area code. A Manhattan phone number should begin with 212, 646 or 917. I didn't know that I'd learned that while I was there but I had. But in a movie, when a New York gumshoe finds a phone number scrawled on the back of a matchbook in a dingy bar, the phone number will *always* begin with 555. Triple five is not a legitimate area code. It's not the code for anywhere in Manhattan. It's not the code for *anywhere* in the US. (There are a few legitimate 555 numbers in existence, but they're for Directory Assistance services, not for people or businesses.)

It has become the convention in America to use 555 for fictional numbers. You can only imagine the trouble they'd cause if they used a number that actually existed. Mind you, you don't have to imagine it because it's happened. In the original release of the 2003 comedy, *Bruce Almighty*, the central character, Bruce (Jim Carrey), is contacted by God (Morgan Freeman – naturally) using the number 776 2323. The film was set in Buffalo so the full number would have been 716 776 2323 and while the producers checked that the full number wasn't in use that didn't help a great deal when the number shown on screen was just 776 2323. (I think this means that God was supposed to be in Buffalo at the time. I guess one of the perks of being omnipresent is that you never have to pay for a long-distance call. But I digress.)

Anyway … plenty of people tried calling the number they saw on the screen to see if they could speak to God and in plenty of other cities in other states, the number was live. In Sanford, North Carolina, it even led to a church where the pastor's first name was Bruce. Oops. By the time the film had been released on DVD they'd managed to change the number. To 555 0123.

555 strikes again.

Once you know about the 555 code it leaps out at you whenever you see it. And often that means you're jolted out of the film. When a film is at its best and you've immersed yourself in its reality, a 555 number is an unwelcome reminder that it's all make-believe. It sets off a klaxon in your head that immediately cuts short any suspension of disbelief. Seeing those three digits on a movie screen is like having someone walk into the cinema, turn on all the lights on and yell, *'Please stop investing any emotional energy in this story. It's not real. You don't need to worry about whether she makes it out alive. She does. She's an actress. I repeat: it is not real.'* They wouldn't be telling you anything you didn't already know … but it's not something you want to be told and it's definitely not *when* you want to be told it.

It gets even more ridiculous when you find out some numbers have been used several times. If you want to call Ghostbusters, you ring 555 2368. But if you Google it, you'll see that the same number was used by Jim Rockford in *The Rockford Files* and Jaime Sommers in *The Bionic Woman*.

Now admittedly those aren't exactly productions where realism is the watchword. There's no real point complaining about being shaken out of a film's reality when that reality involves a giant Stay Puft Marshmallow Man monster. If you can buy the idea that a former tennis pro has been given bionic surgical implants, you can probably cope with the idea that her phone number doesn't exist in the real world. But when the universe created by a production *is* meant to feel real, I for one don't appreciate it when something breaks the spell.

Which brings me to my most recent TV-and-movie bugbear. One that has moved in right next door to 555.

Breaking Bad is, I think, my all-time favourite TV show. It somehow succeeded in making me believe in a down-on-his-luck chemistry teacher's journey into the wild and dangerous world of Class-A drug manufacture. It is impossible to describe the plot without it sounding far-fetched but it is also impossible to watch without getting completely drawn in to Walter White's morally dubious world.

But the threads that hold that belief together are fragile. And in episode two they were broken. In this instance it wasn't because of the old 555. But it *was* phone-number related.

Skyler – Walt's wife – is suspicious about a phone call her husband took at breakfast time. It purported to be a marketing call – and Walt appeared to deal with it as such. But Skyler can't help think there was more to it than that. She can sense that something is up. She's right to be suspicious. It wasn't a marketing call. The call had been made by Jesse Pinkman, Walt's new partner in drug-crime. He'd called in order to discuss – amongst other things – their need to dispose of a dead body. (And this is just episode two. I told you it would sound far-fetched.)

Anyway, Skyler has a phone number. And she wants to know whose phone number it is. The number is 505 148 3369. It's not a 555 number. In fact it's a perfectly convincing phone number for an Albuquerque, New Mexico, address. Not that I thought about that as I watched it for the first time. I didn't think about anything except whether or not Skyler was going to uncover the truth behind Walt's lie. Of course I didn't. Because it was convincing. That's the point. It *isn't* odd. It *isn't* wrong. Nothing jars. And that just serves to pull me a little deeper into the show's world.

Back in that world, Skyler has decided to look the number up. So she does what you or I would do. She opens her laptop. She searches the internet. But she doesn't search the internet in the way that you or I would. Pretty much everyone I know uses Google as their default search engine of choice. I know two or three people who use Bing (and who are really quite insistent that it gives them better, more accurate results). I don't know anyone who uses anything else. I certainly don't know anyone who uses FinderSpyder, but that's the search engine that Skyler turns to. FinderSpyder, of course, doesn't exist.

And that's it. Fake search engines are the new 555. The new spell-breakers. The flip-you-back-to-reality show-spoilers. The reality-klaxons.

But my *Breaking Bad* example broke worse. Because, having discovered Jesse's name, Skyler then clicks through not to Jesse's Myspace but to his myShout profile. You know. That well-known social network: *myShout.US*. What is the point in making the phone numbers convincing if they're immediately going to be fed into a fake search engine to find a fake social network? For me, the show was immediately airlifted from Albuquerque, N.M., to Fakesville, As.If.

This use of a fake internet seems to me to be far worse than Hollywood's widespread 555ism. Because it comes down to pettiness. I can understand why a film producer wants to guarantee that nobody real gets harassed because of a phone number. What would be the equivalent situation if they used Google? No dingbat stoner watching *Breaking Bad* would think, '*Hmmm … I wonder if that website's real… Imma gonna look it up,*' and even if they did … so what? It *is* real. They'll find it. But 300 million people visit it every day. They can handle the extra load.

And what would it matter if a fictional character had a fake profile on a real social networking site? In what way would Myspace be damaged if Jesse Pinkman appeared to be using it? If Jesse Pinkman was real he *would* have used it.

No, the programme makers are forced to break their own reality because of copyright issues. You can't just put Google or Myspace in your TV show! They might sue!

Which is a load of hooey. Because characters in TV shows wear clothes. They drive cars. And they don't invent fake clothing labels and car companies. There isn't an engineering department at the BBC turning out a range of bespoke cars for use in their TV shows so as not to upset the motoring industry's lawyers. They just buy a bloody car! Of course there are cases where the choice of car is a part of some grubby commercial arrangement – a modern *Bond* film is full of product placement – but it's not always the case. When characters in *EastEnders* drive into Albert Square nobody has to seek permission from Ford or Range Rover for deigning to show their design on screen ... so why should Google be treated any differently?

There is something preposterous about a company sending its product out into the big wide world but demanding that nobody is allowed to point a camera at it. But it happens.

On a tour a while ago, I had a stand-up routine that involved me reading a message from the back of a post-card. I used to keep the postcard in the back pocket of my jeans throughout the show and after a few nights' use it would get a little tatty. So every now and then I'd buy a new postcard in whatever town the tour had reached and swap the old one out. I ended up recording a DVD of that show and a few days before the taping, the production manager approached me to tell me we had a problem.

'We don't know if we're going to be able to clear the postcard,' she said, a look of real concern clouding her face.

'What do you mean?'

'We'll probably see a close-up of the postcard. So we need to know who owns the image so we can clear it. And we don't think it's going to be possible.'

'But it's on a postcard,' I said. 'I bought a postcard. I own the postcard. And I'm not doing anything un-postcardy with it. I'm using it as a postcard. I've written a message on it. And I'll be reading that message to an audience. It's a real postcard. It's a real message. I'm a real person. The audience is made up of real people too. I hope. Are you seriously telling me that you're not allowed to film a real person reading a real postcard to some real people?'

'Yes.'

'Shouldn't they have told me that when I bought the postcard? There were no terms and conditions.'

'That's not important. It's the image. It's someone's image.'

'But they sold it to a postcard company. To be used on a postcard. It's on a postcard. I'm using it *as a postcard*. They must have known that other people would use a postcard as a postcard. It's what they do.'

'I'm sorry, Dave. I really am. But I think we're going to have to use a fake postcard.'

'Oh. Of course. Why didn't you say?'

And so that's what we did. And nobody could tell. Because to fake a postcard, you, um … well … you just *make* a postcard. It's just that, in this instance, we made one using a photo I'd taken myself. We obviously trusted me not to sue myself.

Well, I feel the same way about postcards as I do about shoes or cars or chocolate bars or search engines. If real people can use them I think fictional people ought to be able to do the same. I can see that there would be good cause for complaint if, say, a drama wanted to tell you that one of its fictional characters had contracted food poisoning in a real restaurant. Casting fictional aspersions on real entities is obviously a bit dodgy. But what sense is there in preventing fictional people from using your search engine?

Anyone in the world can look at Google's home page free of charge just so long as they have an internet connection. Pretty much everyone in the world who has an internet connection *has* looked at it. There are no background checks in place. Nobody from Google visits your home and interviews your parents to ensure that you're the kind of character they want to be associated with. I can tell you with absolute confidence that many murderers have used Google to, shock–horror, look things up!

Just not in fiction. In fiction, good guys and bad guys alike use FinderSpyder. Or ZapLook. Or EweSearch. Or Search-Wise. Or any of the multitude of others in non-existence.

I've had enough. I want to believe. I want my fiction to *feel* real. I think it's time pretend people were allowed to use the real internet.

CHAPTER 40

• • • • • • • • • • •

TMI

I n Douglas Adams and John Lloyd's peerless book, *The Meaning of Liff*, ordinary place names are repurposed – press-ganged into use as definitions for things there ought to be words for but aren't. So, for example, Sotterley – which is really a village in Suffolk – is given the new meaning of '*the uncovered bit between two shops with awnings, which you have to cross when it's raining.*'

One of my favourite *Liff* definitions is that ascribed to the name of the Irish village, Ahenny:

Ahenny (adj.) The way people stand when examining other people's bookshelves.

I had a moment of sadness the other day when it occurred to me that in the future fewer and fewer people will be standing ahenny. There will, after all, be fewer and fewer bookshelves for us to examine. You can't assess a man's character by looking at the spine of his Kindle. How will we get the measure of a person when their book and record collections are *all* digital? Heavens to Murgatroyd, we might have to go to the trouble of *actually* getting to know them first. Bloody hell.

As everyone knows, you *can* judge a book by its cover … and on public transport we routinely do so – passing judgement not just on the books we see but on the people we see reading them too. But all that disappears in a digital world. Read what you want on the bus. Nobody can judge you. Nobody knows what words the pixels are forming before your eyes. This ought to be liberating in some way. In the digital age, you can show people as much – or as little – of yourself as you like. You have the freedom to be whoever you want to be.

But I'm not sure we want that freedom. I think people *want* to show off who they are. Why else do they share so much of themselves online? I know the intimate details of lives that I'm sure I shouldn't. People I barely know – nice people, people I like but people I worked with once four or five years ago and who I haven't seen since – seem more than happy to share things with the whole of their online friendship circle that they would never volunteer if I bumped into them in the street.

A friend of mine tells a story of a younger relative going on a first date. While the date was in progress he changed his relationship status on Facebook from 'single' to 'in a relationship' and then to 'it's complicated' before posting a message saying something unspeakable about all womankind. All of that happened between the hours of 8pm and midnight. That is definitely an overshare. *That* is too much information.

When I was a kid, a sitcom cliché was the boring character submitting his neighbours to a tedious, post-holiday slideshow of excruciating detail. *'This is Marjorie and me before we boarded the ferry.'* Click. *'This is us boarding the ferry.'* Click. *'This is us having just boarded the ferry.'* Click. *'This is Marjorie browsing in the on-ferry gift shop.'* Click. *'This is Marjorie buying a souvenir snow globe.'* Click. *'This is the souvenir snow globe.'* And so on and so on. In the 70s we dreaded the idea of sitting on someone's sofa while they showed you their holiday snaps but now we sit on our own sofas and scroll through them all on Facebook on our own time. Why?

Many years ago, I sat watching some kind of reality dating show. The idea was that a team of experts set out to transform a long-term singleton into a successful player in the game of romance. The man at the heart of this particular episode was a slightly overweight, self-confessed geek. He was given all sorts of advice designed to make him more confident. He was taught techniques that would help him to feel at ease around women and he was given a crash course in flirting. But he was also given the instruction that on no account should he talk about his collection of comic books and that he must abandon his collection of superhero-themed T-shirts. *'Most women aren't into that stuff,'* he was told. *'You're a nice guy and you don't want to put people off before they've even got to know you.'*

Now, he was a willing participant in the show – and he seemed to appreciate the outcome too – but as a viewer I found myself feeling rather saddened by the whole process. (And it's not because I'm also a slightly over-weight geek. For what it's worth, I have no interest in comic books and only own one superhero-themed T-shirt.)

No, what saddened me was seeing the edges of his personality sanded down. He wanted to find a partner. Why should that involve giving him broad, mass-market appeal? I don't like the idea that he needed to be made more appealing to *more* people, I prefer the idea that he needed to find someone who loved comic books and superheroes just as much as he did. That person might be *harder* to find ... but isn't it better to find the person who fits him than to deny something that was clearly so fundamental to his being?

People aren't houses. You're not supposed to paint them magnolia to make them feel more neutral. We're not supposed to be blank canvasses for someone else to go to work on. We're meant to be ourselves.

If we're not careful, social media can drive us in the same direction. It ought to be liberating. No matter what your quirks and foibles, in the vast expanse of the internet you should be able to find like minds. No one need go without companionship. Nobody needs to feel alone. Nobody needs to paint themselves magnolia.

But when people turn it into a competition – when they count how many friends or followers they have in the same way that we counted up how many Christmas cards we received when we were ten – then the pressure to go for that mass-market neutrality is on. The technology that should have let us seek out like minds ends up encouraging us to seek out any and every mind and to be unhappy when some of them don't want to play.

Why does Twitter send me an email telling me what my 'best' tweet of the week was? Why is it telling me I'd get more followers if I posted more photos? Why is *that* assumed to be everyone's incentive? Can't I be who I am and get whatever I get? Stop trying to cajole me into being someone else.

If a stranger knocked on my door and told me I'd be more popular if I wore a different style of trouser I'd think they were bloody impertinent.

'I don't wear my trousers to be popular,' I'd say, 'they're just the trousers I like. What's it got to do with you?'

'Don't you want to be more popular?' they might say. 'Skinny jeans are in right now.'

'But I don't like skinny jeans. I like comfort. My friends like me. They're not bothered by my trousers. What does it matter what other people think?'

'Well … you know … when you're in the pub … people are sizing you up. They'd like you more if you wore skinny jeans.'

'But I don't go to the pub to appeal to strangers. I go to a pub to hang out with the people I like.'

'Suit yourself.'

Shouldn't we treat Twitter – and the rest of the internet for that matter – the way we treat a pub? It's only supposed to be a place to hang out with the people you like.

EPILOGUE

At the start of this book I posed a question and convention suggests that by the end of the book I ought to be arriving at an answer. I'm supposed to be drawing some kind of conclusion. I'm supposed to offer you solutions. I'm supposed to suggest a way forward.

So, is it all just a load of balls? Yes. And what can we do about it? Nothing.

THE END

*

That doesn't feel very satisfying does it? I guess I should try and offer up a little more.

We live in a world of constant connection and we consume more data than ever before so it's inevitable that we encounter more gobbledegook and googledonk too. Because we encounter more of *everything*. The good, the bad and the ridiculous.

We are natural editors. Without any conscious thought we pick and choose the bits we want (or at least the bits we think we want) and we ignore the rest. The next time you're on a train, spend five minutes watching someone else read a newspaper. Nobody reads one in its entirety from start to finish. They flick through the pages. Their eyes flit about from story to story. They look for the things that interest them and readily dismiss the things that don't. How many of the ads do they read? How many do they take in? Did you read a paper today? How many of the advertisers can you remember? I'm guessing it's not that many. And yet *something* went in. Somehow. Somewhere.

And it's not just newspapers. We consume pretty much all media in the same way. What, if anything, was being advertised on the last website you visited? Was there a banner ad? What was it for?

If you know the answer, the chances are it's because you were annoyed by it. Because it seemed intrusive. Because it did something to override your brain's edit. We don't mind the ads we can ignore. We hate the ones that interrupt.

Maybe we should just carry on ignoring it all? What's the point of examining the world's small print? Who cares if a website regularly misuses the word 'matching' and a newspaper runs the same headline once a week? If game-show contestants being patronised annoys you, don't watch game shows. That's definitely one way to go about it.

But personally I think it is worth trying to slow it all down. I think it is worth making an effort to take more of it in. Because it reframes everything else. When you like something – when you feel persuaded by something – isn't it healthy to stop and ask a few questions. What else do they do? What else do they say? What do they get out of this? Who's advertising here? What does *that* say about them? How smart are they really? Whenever you find yourself admiring the emperor's new clothes, it has to be worth taking a few moments to see if he looks naked from another angle.

So much of the day-to-day data we encounter is informed by tricks, tics, habits and assumptions. Seeing them for what they are has got to be good for us. I like knowing there is idiocy everywhere. It makes me feel less alone.

Can we do anything about it? Probably not. You can't fight the tide, can you?

'To be yourself in a world that is constantly trying to make you something else is the greatest accomplishment'

Ralph Waldo Emerson